SCHOOLHOUSING

*Planning and Designing
Educational Facilities*

FLORA IDA ORTIZ

State University of New York Press

Published by
State University of New York Press, Albany

© 1994 State University of New York

All rights reserved

Printed in the United States of America

No part of this book may be used or reproduced
in any manner whatsoever without written permission
except in the case of brief quotations embodied in
critical articles and reviews.

For information, address the State University of New York Press,
State University Plaza, Albany, NY 12246

Production by Christine Lynch
Marketing by Dana E. Yanulavich

Library of Congress Cataloging-in-Publication Data

Ortiz, Flora Ida.
    Schoolhousing : planning and designing educational facilities /
Flora Ida Ortiz.
      p.   cm.
    Includes bibliographical references and index.
    ISBN 0-7914-1727-1 (alk. paper). — ISBN 0-7914-1728-X (pbk. :
alk. paper)
    1. School buildings—United States—Design and construction.
2. School buildings—United States—Finance. 3. School facilities-
-United States—Design and construction. 4. School facilities-
-United States—Finance. I. Title.
LB3218.A1078 1993
371.6'2'0973—dc20   92-47103
                                                                                               CIP

10 9 8 7 6 5 4 3 2 1

SCHOOLHOUSING

*For my mother, Eliza M. Ortiz,
who provides quiet and constant support to her family.*

Contents

List of Figures	ix
Acknowledgments	xi

PART I. THE CONTEXT

1. School District Project Management	3
2. Schoolhousing	9

PART II. DATA ANALYSIS

3. Preconstruction Considerations	63
4. The Construction of New Schools	103
5. Postconstruction Processes	119
6. The District's Relationship to State Agencies	137
7. Conclusions and Policy Implications	153
References	163
Appendix A: Additional References for Further Reading	181
Author Index	185
Subject Index	189

List of Figures

Figure 1. School Construction and Organizational Functions	17
Figure 2. Linkage to State Agencies	21
Figure 3. School Districts' School Construction Funds Sources	46
Figure 4. School Financing State Agency Involvement	47
Figure 5. Review of the Literature Theoretical Framework	58
Figure 6. Interorganizational and Interpersonal Relationships	146

Acknowledgments

This book has been several years in the making. At its roots lie the need and desire of a number of school superintendents engaged in providing schoolhousing for the increasing number of school children. I am grateful to the California Educational Research Cooperative at the School of Education at the University of California at Riverside and to the superintendents who supported the research process.

Research reported herein was performed pursuant to funds from the California Educational Research Cooperative (CERC) and the University of California at Riverside (UCR). Points of view or opinions stated, however, do not necessarily represent official CERC or UCR positions or policy.

This book would not have been possible without the uncompromising cooperation of all of the CERC school district members. I wish to thank all of those individuals who openly and willingly shared their experiences and knowledge throughout the data collection process. I especially want to thank the facilities planners of each of the school districts examined. Some valuable assistance was also provided to me by the CERC director, manager, other staff members, and CERC fellows. My deeply felt thanks go to them.

I owe an enormous debt to those students who were my research assistants. Edward Nuno, Daniel Morgan, Sandy Gavin, and Janet Sisneros participated as graduate research assistants and CERC fellows. Undergraduates, Chandra Thompson, Alice Garcia, and Ainez Chong, as part of the Minority Summer Research Internship Program, collected and transcribed data for me. These students' efforts are sincerely appreciated.

Throughout the preparation of this book I have benefitted from comments and suggestions of a number of friends and colleagues. Douglas Mitchell read early versions of the manuscript and gave both encouragement and advice. I especially want to thank Robert Jorgensen and Jean Treiman for providing reactions and reassurances after reviewing the entire manuscript.

Thanks are due to my sister, Frances Ortiz, for entering half of the manuscript into the computer. Finally, I want to thank my niece, Karla Goltman, for assistance in editing, proofing, and final assembly of the document.

Part I

The Context

Chapter 1

School District Project Management

INTRODUCTION

This book is about how, when, and why public school districts build new schools. All organizations, at one time or another, undertake major projects. For school districts, the most complex, comprehensive, visible, and enduring project they undertake is the planning and designing of school facilities. This activity occurs periodically, sometimes as infrequently as every two decades. This periodic aspect to the process means that school districts are seldom prepared to assume the responsibility in terms of in-house experience or resources. Thus, when school districts engage in constructing new schools, a project other than regular school district business has to be accommodated. The process of building school facilities requires project management from the school districts' organization.

At the present time, the national and international needs for educational facilities are grave. New growth, aging facilities, and population displacement are occurring on a worldwide scale, requiring school facilities of one kind or another. The American Association of School Administrators (AASA), representing 18,500 of the nation's school superintendents and other top administrators, reports that replacement of 74 percent of the nation's school buildings built prior to World War II or during the 50s-60s era of cheap construction to meet "Baby Boom" needs is overdue. Twelve percent of the buildings are considered inadequate; they are too old, too small, have deteriorating mechanical systems, or seriously need window replacement. Eleven percent of the nation's schools have been built since 1980 (American Association of School Administrators, 1991).

Teens across the nation place building maintenance and construction as their number one priority, whereas adults place it in fourteenth place. A 1988 study by the Carnegie Foundation for the Advancement of Teaching reports that students' attitudes about education are a direct reflection of their learning environment. An independent study of the Washington, D.C. schools released in the summer of 1991 concluded that city kids could do 5-11 percent better on standardized tests if the physical conditions of their schools improved (USA Weekend, 1991; American Association of School Administrators, 1991). The AASA (1991) concluded that there is a serious leadership void at the federal level and in most states in regard to the provision of facilities or facility guidance.

Even though this report is based on California school districts, school construction is an activity taking place in other areas of the world and the nation. Across the nation, the organizing unit that assumes responsibility for the project is the school district. The activities include initiating, acquiring funds for construction, and terminating the project.

The issues that demand attention are:

1. The reorganization of the school district structure in order to embark on a project
2. The search for expert and special knowledge and skills outside the organization in order to complete the project
3. The solicitation of community support for the facility
4. The solicitation of funds in order to complete the project
5. The development of working relationships with a variety of regulatory agencies
6. The coordination of all parties throughout the process
7. The management of the project from inception to completion
8. The solicitation of continuing support and ownership of the facility after completion

School facility construction provides an opportunity to examine how organizations reorganize themselves to manage projects. Examining California school construction provides an opportunity to see how multiple projects are handled, inasmuch as many of the districts under study were constructing more than one school. The *how* specifies the school's reorganization and the steps necessary to the process.

Special projects require support and specialized technical help from outside the school district. How do organizations integrate outside specialists and experts in the conduct of a project? What are the components of the relationship and who is responsible for initiating, maintaining, and terminating the relationship? Public school construction also requires state agency approval. These agencies regulate and provide funds and other types of technical support. The relationship with these agencies is ongoing throughout the construction process, making it necessary that the character of the relationship be understood. The *who* constructs new schools includes the school district's personnel, specialists from outside the organization, and regulators from state and local agencies.

Two factors that trigger school districts' educational facilities construction are replacement of buildings and enrollment increases due to new development and population shifts. For example, in the state of California enrollment increases have resulted from both new development and new groups of immigrants. School planners relying on the California State Department of Finance's Demographic Research Unit were dismayed at the prediction of 556,000 babies in 1990 when the National Center for Health Statistics reported that 310,000 children arrived in the first six months. The assistant state superintendent for school facilities planning in California said, "In terms of our planning, we are $6 billion in the hole already. There are people that, halfway serious, halfway facetiously, are talking about tents" (Lewis, 1990, p. A-3). The two fastest growing counties in the state of California project dramatic increases. The county of Riverside is expected to increase enrollment from 201,600 in 1989 K-12 to 417,100 in 1999 K-12, a growth of 106.95 percent; and San Bernardino County is expected to increase from 268,300 in 1989 K-12 to 513,700 in 1999 K-12, a growth of 91.46 percent (Heydt, 1991).

Associated with increased enrollments and the need for school-housing is the need for funds to support the building. In California, the typical cost of new construction, which includes site preparation, architects' fees, furniture and equipment, and construction, is about $125 a square foot. The typical school construction cost, excluding land, is $4.5 million for elementary, $10 million for junior or middle high, and $23 million for high school. The land costs vary greatly, but they tend to average about 25 percent of the total project cost. The state limits are 10 percent. The sobering conclusion is, thus, that even using the lower state projections, districts need more than $12.5 billion over the next five years.

School construction becomes necessary *when* students can no longer be accommodated in the existing facilities, *when* the use of relocatables has been exhausted, and *when* a source of funds for the construction has been identified.

Schoolhousing construction differs from other types of projects in that the purpose of the facility is loaded with symbolic and moral overtones. The facility is meant to house children, to be a place where learning takes place, and to symbolize the community's deeply held values. The *why* to construct new facilities is that children need to be housed in order to be educated. But beyond that, the facility must be a school that reflects the value placed on children, learning, safety, and aesthetics in order to fulfill its function. School buildings are, thus, the safest buildings in a community, and the most available during disasters. In brief, the construction of schools differs from other projects because it embodies community values and accessibility to children for education, evaluation, and shelter.

This report is organized into two major sections. Chapter I includes the introduction and the methodology used in the study. Chapter II covers the review of the literature and the formulation of the theoretical framework. The second section is the analysis of the data. Chapter III analyzes the steps prior to the construction of the building. Chapter IV deals with the construction process. Chapter V presents the postconstruction process, and Chapter VI examines the relationship of the school district to the state agencies. Chapter VII presents the conclusions and policy implications.

METHODOLOGY

This study dealing with schoolhousing was requested by twenty school district California Educational Research Cooperative (CERC) member superintendents. School enrollment in the Inland Empire has continuously increased, requiring additional school facilities. The issues of concern for the CERC superintendents were: How can school facilities be best provided for school children? What resources are available for school construction? What financial plans are most appropriate and how can we judge whether school facilities are being built in the best possible way? The research question, How are school districts providing schoolhousing for children in California? became the focus. Other questions emerged as the project got under way: What are the phases a project goes through before completion? Who are the key participants involved in the process? and, How do they enact their roles?

The investigation into these questions began by trying to determine how many school buildings were being constructed in the area. The Office of Local Assistance (OLA) provided general information, and it was determined that in the area covered by the CERC member districts over one hundred schools were at different phases of the construction process.

These school districts were contacted to determine which official was responsible for building schoolhouses. Most school districts were found to have appointed facilities planners. Some school districts assigned the responsibility of facilities to their associate superintendent of finance and budgeting. Small school districts had their superintendents in charge of school facility planning.

All school facilities planners and/or district personnel responsible for facility planning were interviewed. From the data gathered, a small sample of six school districts was selected for extensive study. Four districts were examined in detail and the remaining two were used for comparison as necessary. The districts differed in size, methods of building new schools, degree of community involvement, and community characteristics.

Data were collected through interviews, observation, and document analysis. From the selected districts, a sample of individuals representing the districts and area of involvement was selected to be interviewed. The individuals chosen were likely to be principals, teachers, school board members, superintendents, parents, custodians, architects, contractors, and others who were involved in one way or another with the construction of school facilities. State agency officials were also interviewed.

Data collected through observation included school activities and functions related to school construction. Photographs were taken to record the progress of some school sites. Notes were compiled from films from the Lloyds Laboratories Incorporated and D. G. King Associates, *Demographics for California School Construction Funding, Simplified* and a lecture film, *Financing New School Construction*, presented by an instructor.

Document analysis included reviewing newspaper accounts and other media reports of school building issues. Technical reports, such as school district manuals on financing and school site selection, as well as long-range programs, architects designs, state legal documents, and agency rules and regulations, were collected and analyzed.

Meetings held by agencies such as the State Allocation Board (SAB) and the county facilities planners were attended for the collection of observation, interview, and document data. The Coalition for Adequate School Housing (CASH) conference, the School Legal Defense Association (SLDA) conference, and other local organizational meetings were also attended for the same purpose.

The theoretical framework applied to the analysis was derived from the literature review and the data. After extensive categorization and classification of data entries, concepts and constructs were generated to explain relationships uncovered in the data. Four major parts to a theoretical framework emerged: (1) the identification of the fundamental steps in the process of constructing school facilities, (2) the classification of organizational functions, (3) the basis for the school district's relationship to the state agencies, and (4) the interorganizational and interpersonal relationships between the school district and state agency officials.

The chapter that follows is the review of the literature and the formulation of the theoretical framework presented on pages 14-25.

Chapter 2

Schoolhousing

INTRODUCTION

New school buildings are produced through a complex sequence of events. The process begins with the identification of space needs, entails extensive school district planning and organizing, and ends with certification of the completed school. Though the process varies widely from district to district, many different individuals and groups are typically involved. In addition to district staff, state agency officials are always involved. Most school districts involve those who are directly responsible for the planning and construction of the school building. Many districts take pains to involve community leaders and parent groups.

While ideological conflicts and policy debates are certainly not rare, most participants approach school construction as an essentially practical but complex problem. Success in raising funds, securing adequate technical assistance, and winning broad community support are essential to defining needs and completing facility construction. Constructing a school is not simply a school district governance decision; it is a kind of activity that demands public support and district accountability as well as expert and technical knowledge, skill, and leadership.

FACTORS AFFECTING NEW SCHOOLHOUSING

The complex process of planning and constructing new schools produces much more than physical housing for children. It makes a vital symbolic statement about community values and educational philosophy. This symbolic role makes facility construction one of the most important responsibilities of any local district because facility decisions have enduring consequences for students and community alike.

A major factor shaping the construction process is the social interaction among district staff and the staff of state agencies with funding and regulatory authority over the process. These interactions are shaped by competing educational philosophies and impact sharply on the definitions of schoolhousing needs as well as shape the way construction priorities are perceived and pursued. Since community growth tends to precede schoolhousing construction, construction planning typically unfolds in a stressful and often turbulent environment.

THE DEMAND FOR SCHOOLHOUSING

California provides a dramatic example of the cyclical nature of educational facilities need. According to estimates provided by Bill Honig (Heydt, 1991, no page), the State Superintendent of Instruction in California, "close to five million students now attend California public schools, and approximately 1.5 million new students will enter our schools during the next five years." State projections (Heydt, 1991) indicate that 1,277 new schools, or over 35,000 new classrooms, will be called for to house expanding enrollment by 1995.

The ever-increasing demand for fiscal resources to provide adequate school housing has resulted in a number of state appropriations. Over the last five years, California voters have passed bond issues totaling $950 million. The California Legislature has appropriated an additional $750 million from tidelands oil revenues. The appropriations are, however, insufficient to meet the need. One estimate is that the state requires $12.65 billion more in order to provide adequate schoolhousing for its youth (Heydt, 1991). The California educational system, as other systems across the nation, is seriously challenged by the need to generate adequate schoolhousing with scarce resources.

A RECENT HISTORY OF SCHOOLHOUSING

California, as well as other states, used legislation and court decisions to alter the system by which school districts build schools. For example, in California the *Serrano v. Priest* (1974) court decision mandating state equalization of school funding had already started to direct financing for school facilities to the state level with the passage of Proposition 13. School districts that had previously financed school construction with local board money or by borrowing from the state were generally unable to secure the required two-thirds vote from the district voters. The decline in local funding that followed passage of Proposition 13 necessitated legislative revision of the State School Building Lease-Purchase Act so that districts could receive state aid for financing local school construction without having to return funds to the state. Under the revised plan, districts receive "quasi grants." The state pays for the construction of new school facilities and rents them for a nominal fee ($1 per year plus any interest earned on state construction money) to local school districts under a long-term lease-purchase agreement. Title to the facilities is transferred to the individual districts no later than 40 years after the rental agreement has been executed.

INVOLVEMENT OF STATE AGENCIES

State agencies become involved in the process of planning, designing, and constructing new schools in order to regulate and fund the process and ensure that safe facilities are built. The state of California provides an example of how these state agencies relate to school districts. Four state agencies are involved in the process of planning, designing, and constructing new schools; however, no one agency has total responsibility for the process. The State Allocation Board (SAB) is a legislatively appointed body, which was first created in 1950. The board is composed of the Director of Finance, the Superintendent of Public Instruction, the Director of General Services, two senators, and two assemblymen. This body's responsibilities are to receive all applications for state funding from local districts and to make the final allotments.

One of the two offices located in the Department of General Services is the Office of Local Assistance (OLA), which is responsible for processing these applications and bringing recommendations for fund authorization to SAB. The second office is the Office of the State Architect (OSA), which is responsible for school design and architectural integrity. OSA assures that plans meet building code requirements, are earthquake safe, comply with space authorization limits, and meet other technical specifications. The California State Department of Education's School Facility Planning Division (CSDE/SFPD) reviews building designs to determine whether they meet criteria for educational soundness. This unit assures a proper mix of classroom, laboratory, and other learning environments, as well as a balance between instructional and noninstructional components. All school construction approval, regardless of the funding source, necessitates school district interaction with CSDE/SFPD) and OSA. These agencies enforce compliance with a wide variety of procedural and planning requirements. OLA and SAB enter the process when school districts apply for state funding.

AN EXAMINATION OF AGENCY REGULATIONS AND PRACTICES

The process required to construct school facilities has evolved into a system of regulations and requirements imposed by the four state agencies. In response to school districts' complaints about the ever-increasing complexities and delays, the California Legislature commissioned the accounting firm of Price-Waterhouse (1988) to investigate the California school construction regulations and practices and recommend ways to simplify and accelerate the process. The Price-Waterhouse firm based its study on the premise that the ultimate goal for the state is to fund adequate school facilities where and when needed. The report's explanation of apparent delays and complexities in the building of new schools focused attention on the differences between state and local interests.

The state's agenda for school construction has five characteristics: (1) maximizing the number of basic or simple school classrooms that can be built from available funds, (2) making facility construction a last-resort option after maximum use of existing and temporary facilities has been assured, (3) maximizing the amount of local funding made available for all projects, (4) minimizing the risk that "unneeded" projects will be approved, and (5) minimizing the risk that a variety of state policies will be violated due to school district negligence or abuse.

Local school district interests have four characteristics, two of which are directly at odds with state interests: (1) maximizing the amount of state funding and (2) minimizing district contributions to facility construction. The other two local interests, though not directly at odds with state priorities, complicate the local/state relationship: (3) building facilities that respond to local requirements and (4) avoiding community conflicts over site selection and use of surplus schools.

The differences between state and local agendas are reconciled through three different mechanisms used by the state to shape construction of school facilities. First, the state *regulates the process* by which schools are planned and constructed. Second, it *establishes priorities* and funds school design and construction work. Third, the state provides a variety of *support services* aimed at helping school districts deal with planning and compliance problems.

The reconciliation of state and local agendas is problematic, however. The Price-Waterhouse report identified three major obstacles to efficient planning and construction of school facilities. The first obstacle is the fragmented structure displayed by the state. CSDE/SFPD, OSA,

OLA, and SAB are each responsible for a different policy area (educational policy, building safety, and efficient use of limited financial resources, respectively). The second obstacle is the administrative weaknesses within the state agencies. The major weaknesses are: a lack of formal internal operating policy and procedures manuals in all offices at the state level; lack of adequate computer support, which exacerbates problems related to document control and filing systems, lack of adequate application and workload monitoring systems, and cumbersome property check procedures. The third obstacle identified by Price-Waterhouse is administrative failings at the school district level. The report underscores the importance of insufficient advance planning by districts and a shortage of qualified project managers.

IMPLEMENTATION OF PRICE-WATERHOUSE RECOMMENDATIONS

Based on their findings, Price-Waterhouse made several recommendations that were intended to strengthen OLA; redirect CSDE/SFPD to training, planning, and research activities; and direct OSA to provide school districts with estimates of how long the approval process should take for a low-cost plan, a medium-cost plan, and a high-cost plan.

Responses to the Price-Waterhouse report and recommendations were described in an SAB report (State Allocation Board, 1989). Of the nine recommendations made to OLA, seven were immediately implemented. The remaining two—replacing the traditional method of projecting enrollments with an alternative method (counting teaching stations) and using standardized building plans to conserve both architectural development and plan review resources—were later approved by SAB and implemented.

Five of the nine Price-Waterhouse recommendations were directed toward CSDE/SFPD. CSDE/SFPD concurred with two: (1) elimination of the five-year plan requirement from the application process, and (2) shifting CSDE/SFPD focus to overall facility planning, development of training materials and programs for district personnel, and conducting research and evaluation studies of state programs' impact on school districts. It did not concur with the recommendations to eliminate the plan review and approval steps from the application process, and to eliminate the site acquisition review and approval step. CSDE/SFPD suggested an alternative provision for the fifth recommendation. Instead of providing school districts with facilities, consulting services, and training through six regional school facilities planning offices, CSDE/SFPD proposed establishing educational facilities planning centers operating in cooperation with one or more colleges or universities.

This recommendation would have created the equivalent of the School Planning Laboratory located at Stanford University between 1950 and 1977. That laboratory, as part of the Stanford School of Education, studied such topics as building, furniture, and equipment design; space utilization; facility maintenance; business management; learning environments; and population projections. Until its demise in 1977, the Laboratory published research findings and provided technical assistance to local districts (Boice, 1968; Educational Facilities Laboratories, 1967; Palmer, 1975). It had neither formal authority over district construction decisions nor explicit responsibility to state agencies.

The Price-Waterhouse recommendations directed toward OSA emphasized the need for expediting decisions and simplifying and streamlining procedures. Two recommendations to OSA were accepted. OSA agreed to establish separate plan-checking turnaround standards and time schedules for low-, medium-, and high-cost plans, and to utilize OLA application numbers in conjunction with OLA projects in order to facilitate project tracking. A procedure was adopted to identify OLA application numbers and funding status and to acknowledge these numbers in a letter to OLA.

School district-state agency relationships have been strengthened through the implementation of various Price-Waterhouse recommendations. The focus of this relationship is now more directly on the SAB/OLA funding process. The proposed shift from regulation to provision of support and service in OSA and CSDE/SFPD did not materialize, however. Both OSA and CSDE/SFPD retain a substantial regulatory emphasis on their relations with local districts. In order to understand the dynamics of state influence and to interpret the processes of local-district facility planning and construction, a comprehensive review was undertaken. A theoretical framework for synthesizing that literature is presented in the next section.

TOWARD A THEORETICAL ANALYSIS OF SCHOOL FACILITY CONSTRUCTION

Analysis of the available literature on school facility construction is driven by two questions. First, what tensions tend to develop among the key actors at various steps during the process of design, construction, and schoolbuilding occupancy? Second, what are the typical conflicts of interest in orientation among executive leaders, professional experts, and political representatives participating in these processes?

The traditional means for addressing the issue of schoolhousing has been to decide how to build school facilities as the need arises. Since neither public nor professional interest has been high except during periods of acute facility shortage, the literature tends to reflect the most common and obvious elements. According to the 18th Annual Gallup Poll (1985), only 1 percent of the respondents considered lack of proper facilities as a problem facing the schools. There was virtually a total lack of interest in school facilities among the numerous school-reform reports generated during the 1980s (Council of Educational Facility Planners, 1986b). John Goodlad's *A Place Called School* (1984), for example, makes no reference to the physical facilities. Theodore Sizer, in *Horace's Compromise* (1984), makes oblique reference to facilities in the assertion that "human factors" rather than physical ones shape the climate of the school.

Although there was a lack of interest in school facilities, three reports do address the issue. Ernest Boyer's *High School: A Report on Secondary Education in America* (1983) refers to school facilities a number of times. For example, in his description of Ridgefield High School, he writes of the "two-story brick building built in the 1930s now showing its years and lack of care" (p. 11) and urban schools "with wire-covered windows and graffiti-covered walls" (p. 16). The *Carnegie Report* (Tucker and Mandel, 1986) recommends schools depart from the "egg-crate" style of classroom construction, and the National Governor's Association Report (Alexander and Keen, 1986) discusses technical assistance for school districts. The latter report specifies that building programs, year-round schooling, and the establishment of policies for the disposal of obsolete buildings be part of their deliberations, as well as construction, restoration, and multiple use of school buildings.

It is evident that school-building construction is a multi-billion dollar business. Leu (1965, p. 1) writes that "the value of our existing school plans is roughly estimated to be four times the assets of our nation's largest corporation." The demand for additional schoolhousing is rising at the same time that procedures for funding and constructing are becoming more complex. As a result, it is increasingly important that the processes involved in the construction of schools be examined and understood.

Four key ideas form the foundation for the theoretical framework to be used in this review. The first idea, borrowed from Herbert Kaufman (1956), emphasizes the characteristic form and persistent tension among three basic governmental functions: executive leadership, professional expertise, and representative legitimacy. As the literature review unfolds, the influence of these three core governmental functions on the state and local educational officials will be apparent.

The second idea needed to form an adequate theory of school facility development is the recognition of stages or steps in the school facility planning, construction, and utilization processes. The framework developed in this report delineates nine distinct steps in the process and describes how the executive, professional, and representational functions differ as facility development moves from one step to the next.

The third basic idea incorporated in this theoretical framework was provided by Theodore Lowi (1971, 1979, 1964, 1985a, 1985b; Lowi and Stone, 1978), who reported the critical differences between "regulatory," "distributive," and "redistributive" governmental policies as they affect the actions of local officials and ordinary citizens. The school facility planning and construction process is conditioned by the state/local relationships, which may be based on the regulatory authority of the state or the redistributive effects of technical or other types of support.

Finally, the schoolhousing development process requires attention to the character and impact of interpersonal relationships that develop between the local school district officials and the various state and local agency leaders as they interact with each other. The structure and operations of the schoolhousing construction process in California create interpersonal tension between the local school staff and the state officials as local officers seek fiscal aid and procedural approval. Concepts from Goldberg (1983) are useful in describing the interorganizational tensions, and concepts from Walton (1972) and Evan (1972) present the interpersonal dilemmas facing school district officers. Vertical interdependence (Goldberg, 1983) places school districts in a dependent relationship with state agencies. The instrumental and expressive meanings (Walton, 1972; Evan, 1972) that school officials and state agency officers bring to the interaction create identity conflict for school officials. They resolve this conflict by avoiding the interaction. Figure 1 shows the relationship between the first two key ideas in the theoretical framework developed for this report.

THE THREE FUNCTIONS

The columns of Figure 1 distinguish among the three competing functional values outlined in Herbert Kaufman's essay. Representativeness relates to the adequacy with which all legitimate interests are incorpo-

FIGURE 1
School Construction and Organizational Functions

Steps	Executive	Professional	Representative
1. Needs Assessment	Initiative	Demographic Analysis	Recognition
2. Long-Range Plan	Organization	Advisory	Legitimacy/ Direction
3. Fiscal Plan	Decision Making	Technical Assistance	Mobilize Support
4. Building Design	Integration	Technical Assistance	Preference/ Representation
5. Contract Bidding	Authorization	Expertise	Legitimation
6. Construction	Supervision	Technical	Approval/ Support
7. Occupy Building	Leadership	Administration	Support
8. Evaluate	Judgment	Inspection	Accountability
9. Building Use	Negotiation	Advice	Advocacy

rated into the scope and content of public service programs. Neutral competence is "to do the work of government expertly, and to do it according to explicit, objective standards rather than to personal or party or other obligations and loyalties" (p. 1060). Executive leadership is the degree to which an organization is assured that coordination systems and service operations are capable of critical task performance in a timely and cost-efficient manner.

Kaufman writes, "Each of these values has been dominant (but not to the point of total suppression of the others) in different periods of our history; the shift from one to another generally appears to have occurred as a consequence of the difficulties encountered in the period preceding the change" (p. 1057). To illustrate, the first third of the twentieth century gave rise to a political system in which the dominance of representativeness as a criteria for public service organization and delivery resulted in "bossism," in local government. Political bosses, "while providing a measure of integration in the bewildering pullulation of government, often utilized their positions to advance their personal interests and the interests of the organizations they headed without regard for the interests of many of the governed" (pp. 1059-60). As disillusionment with the bossiness of overdeveloped representative systems sets in, a "clean-up" period aimed at removing the politics from the process and relying more on experts led to the replacement of the representative function with the neutral competence function.

Unfortunately, when control is turned over to politically neutral and professionally competent experts, the decision-making process becomes fragmented and agencies begin to pursue contradictory policies in related fields. The neutral competence function "create[s] a thrust toward fragmentation within government, toward the formation of highly independent islands of decision-making occupied by officials who [go] about their business without much reference to each other or to other organs of government" (Kaufman, p. 1062). Strong executive leadership is needed to bring this problem under control. Throughout history the reformers turned to the chief executives to rationalize the spending process, and out of this came the now familiar phenomena of executive review and adjustment of agency requests and the submittal of comprehensive budgets delineating overall spending patterns (p. 1064). As officials and agencies become more accomplished in their respective areas of specialization, however, they tend to resent efforts of "laymen" and "amateurs" to exercise control. Thus, executive domination has the effect of weakening representatives along with corralling the experts. The result is a contest over the limits of executive authority.

When Kaufman's analysis of the interrelation of functions in the field of public administration is applied to the processes of planning, building, and opening new school facilities, it appears evident that it is natural for officials representing each of the three basic functions to experience tensions and conflict regarding who should have ultimate control over various steps in the process. It is inevitable that some individuals with responsibility for either representative or neutral competence functions will step forward to challenge the authority of the executive and attempt to assume some of the executive's responsibilities and that some executives will relinquish power to them. Smooth and efficient completion of tasks and transition from one step to the next in the planning and building process requires that the three competing functions become integrated and maintain an appropriate balance in their respective domains. To ensure stability and consistency, the executive function will permeate the entire planning, construction, and opening process. The representative and neutral competence functions operate when called upon by the executive. They move in and out of the various steps, performing their appropriate tasks.

The *executive function* is usually carried out by the superintendent, associate superintendent for business, and/or a facilities planner. This executive assumes responsibility for the total planning and construction operation, including such activities as coordination of policies across fields and agencies, the designation of jurisdictional spheres, determination of areas of service and regulation, and supervision across areas of activities.

The *representative function* is fulfilled by the school board, community representatives, and the leadership of educational organizations and other interested parties. Formally, the school board, representing the community, presents input to school district executives, certifies the need for new facilities, and approves the process by which the facilities are to be built. Special-interest-group representatives provide input to the board or directly to school district executives in order to have their desires incorporated into the process of school construction.

The *professional function* is fulfilled by various specialists and experts with specific technical, legal, and fiscal knowledge. Persons who fill this role include architects, contract lawyers, engineers, and educators. As an example, the architect designs the buildings, but educators specify the details that serve to insure that the building is a school. The lawyers provide legal assistance in contract and bidding procedures. Engineers provide technical assistance, such as installation of utility and communication lines.

CONSTRUCTION PROCESS STEPS

Shown in the rows of Figure 1 are the nine distinctive steps involved in planning and constructing new school facilities:

1. Assessment of demographic changes and facility needs
2. Long-range planning for new facilities
3. Fiscal planning for provisions of resources and financing construction
4. Site selection, development of educational specifications, and design of architectural features for the planned facility
5. Development, bidding, and letting of contracts for facility construction

6. Construction of the building
7. Occupying the building through staffing and programming
8. Postoccupancy evaluation of building and securing of needed alterations
9. Facility utilization

These nine specific steps constitute the process. Depending on the various analysts' frames of reference, these steps are sometimes condensed into as few as three basic activities (Engelhardt, 1970) or as many as fifty-four separate steps, as identified in the Price-Waterhouse Report (1988). As explained above, the nine steps delineated here remain distinct because each step requires a different configuration of the three organizational functions. The specific content of these nine basic steps and the extent to which each has been the object of significant school construction research will be reviewed in the main body of this report, following a brief sketch of the history of school construction in America (see page 25).

INTERPRETING STATE/LOCAL RELATIONSHIPS

School construction is not performed autonomously by the local school districts. They must cooperate with and be accountable to many external agencies. State agencies are ultimately responsible for adequate schoolhousing. These agencies regularly interact with local district officials in authorizing, designing, and financing school facilities. As noted earlier, in California the four state agencies are the State Allocation Board (SAB), the Office of Local Assistance (OLA), the California State Department of Education/State Facilities Planning Division (CSDE/SFPD), and the Office of the State Architect (OSA).

As suggested by the entries in Figure 2, relationships between the four prominent agencies and local district officials can be described by applying Theodore Lowi's concepts: regulatory, distributive, and redistributive (Lowi, 1964, 1971, 1979, 1985a, 1985b; Lowi and Stone, 1978). Without distorting Lowi's original concepts, the more meaningful phrases "support" and "fiscal" will refer respectively to Lowi's distributive and redistributive categories. This is useful in this context because the state agencies have no independent sources of money. They can only provide resources through taxation or the diversion of funds from other purposes. The fiscal allocations are thus redistributive. Lacking money to allocate, distributive agencies provide technical or symbolic support.

According to Lowi, whenever public policy actions are primarily concerned with imposing procedures or controlling specific actions,

FIGURE 2
Linkage to State Agencies

Process	SAB (OLA)	OSA	CSDE
1. Request for Application	Regulatory		Distributive
2. Approve Application	Regulatory Redistributive		Distributive
3. Approve Fiscal Plan	Regulatory Redistributive		Distributive
4. Approve Site, Design, & Specifications	Regulatory	Regulatory	Regulatory Distributive
5. Approve Bid	Regulatory		
6. Award Contract	Regulatory Redistributive		
7. Occupy Building			Distributive
8. Evaluate			Distributive
9. Building Use			Distributive

they define the state/local relationship as one that is primarily "regulatory" in character. In the case of school construction, this regulatory relationship confronts local districts with demands for adherence to rules, regulations, procedures, and standards. When state agencies use the taxing authority of the state to raise money for particular local projects, the relationship is redistributive; that is, money is taken from some tax payers to be put at the disposal of others.

The third state/local relationship takes place when state authority is used to give local access to resources not raised through taxation. While Lowi emphasized allocation of public land and resources, his "distributive" concept applies to state offers of authoritative legitimacy, technical assistance, or symbolic support to various local projects. State support for local action and initiative plays an important role in encouraging and directing local district facilities development. The term *symbolic support* is used here to characterize state initiatives that encourage local direction without redirecting public resources.

Though regulatory and fiscal policies differ, they share one characteristic between them: the use of coercive power to assure compliance with their intent. State agencies, by applying these policies, coercively control school district facility construction activities. Tax and bond money raised from the general taxpaying public is allocated to school districts when they meet specific criteria and follow complex, often convoluted procedures.

In schooling, as in other policy arenas, the sequence is as follows:

> A program is authorized and an administrative agency is put into operation to work without legal guidelines through an elaborate, sponsored bargaining process in which the broad area monopolized by the government [state] is given back piece by piece as a privilege to specific individuals or groups [local school districts] on a case-by-case basis (often called "on the merits"). (Lowi, 1979, p. 278)

The third link between the the state and the local school district fits the pattern described by Lowi as "distribution" policies. The state has control over an abundance of information and is able to provide information and technical assistance to the school district during the planning and construction process. Because the state is able to provide such services, the district is inclined to adopt a dependency relationship and seek symbolic legitimation as well as information and technical support services (Lowi, 1964; 1971; 1979; 1985a; 1985b; Lowi and Stone, 1978; Dunham and Marmar, 1978).

During the first six steps of the school facilities development process, the relationship between districts and the state tends to be dominated by regulatory and fiscal concerns. During steps seven through nine, the relationship tends to shift toward the symbolic legitimation and technical support forms of interaction. Supportive relationships often develop during the earlier steps, especially if local districts nurture the relationship by actively pursuing information, training services, advice, and approval.

THE INTERPERSONAL DIMENSIONS OF FACILITY CONSTRUCTION

The relationship between the school district and the state agencies is conducted at two levels: interorganizationally and interpersonally.

Interorganizationally, the relationship is vertically interdependent (Goldberg, 1983; Pennings, 1981, 1978; Pennings and Goodman, 1977). Vertical interdependence exists among organizations that are located at adjacent stages of a production process (Goldberg, p. 108). The magnitude of this relationship is "a function of the substitutability and criticalness of the resources involved. Criticalness refers to the importance of the resources in the sense that discontinuation of their flow would impede the focal organization's functioning" (Goldberg, p. 109). As state control over facility construction financing has increased, vertical interdependence between local districts and the state agencies has also gone up. Moreover, vertical interdependence is most prominent in the relationship between districts and SAB and OLA, the agencies with direct fiscal control.

The interpersonal aspects of this relationship also need to be understood, however, in order to present a complete picture of these working relationships. On most issues, interorganizational interaction involves only a part of the personnel. Interactions among the individuals involved take on both instrumental and expressive meanings (Walton, 1972). Instrumentally, bureaucratic procedures are developed and controlled by the state. At the expressive level, procedures are evaluated and credit or blame is allocated by participants to various staff or to the agencies themselves. Since the district staff is at greater risk (failure to secure resources or authorization is highly traumatic for the district staff) it also tends toward greater expressive reactions to these transactions.

The institutions possess identities, statuses, or images that their members want to establish or maintain. The individual interpersonal relationships may reinforce that identity or may cause identity conflict. In the case of identity conflict, avoidance of the interaction may take place (see Evan, 1972). Successful engagement in a social relationship depends on creating and sustaining a "definition of the situation" that gives a reasonable account of motives and actions. The "situation" in which individuals from the school district interact with individuals from the state agencies is one of vertical interdependence between the two, an interdependence in which the school district personnel are cast in a subordinate role. Incongruently, the individuals involved typically occupy hierarchically important positions in their own organizations, making this dependency relationship doubly uncomfortable. The result is the tendency to redefine the situation in formalistic ways, with the individuals relating to each other in instrumental rather than expressive ways. When expressive communication does emerge, it is likely to reinforce identity conflict and encourage school officials to avoid further interaction.

One typical avoidance strategy is for senior school district officials to delegate their responsibilities to lower ranking support staff members. This relieves expressive conflict, but threatens the clarity and timeliness of communication.

THEORETICAL FRAMEWORK SUMMARY

The theoretical framework for analyzing school facility construction processes can be summarized in four key ideas. First, school districts follow a process which consists of nine fundamental steps: (1) needs assessment; (2) long-range planning; (3) fiscal planning; (4) school building planning, which includes school site planning and selection, architectural services, and educational specifications; (5) bidding for contractors; (6) constructing the building; (7) occupying the building; (8) postoccupancy evaluation; and (9) school building use.

Second, school districts accomplish these nine steps by coordinating three functions: executive leadership, professional expertise, and representative legitimation. The executive function provides procedural order and allocation of resources. The professional function provides specialized and expert knowledge and skill. The representative function balances attention between special interests and the common good. Each operational function resolves specific problems during each of the nine steps.

Third, in order for the school district to construct new schools, it is also necessary to relate to external agencies such as the state. The basis for this relationship is threefold: regulation, fiscal allocation, and technical or symbolic support distribution. The regulatory relationship is based on adhering to rules, regulations, procedures, and standards imposed by the state. The fiscal relationship is based on state control over design and construction funds.

The state/local relationship is focused on the four separate agencies described earlier: SAB, OLA, CSDE/SFPD, OSA. The district's basis for relating to SAB and OLA is largely regulatory and fiscal, although technical assistance is also sought. The district's basis for relating to OSA is almost entirely regulatory. The district's basis for relating to CSDE/SFPD tends to be regulatory, but often includes the distribution of technical and symbolic support.

Fourth, local school district and state officials relate to each other interpersonally as well as interorganizationally. The interorganizational relationship creates vertical interdependence (Goldberg, 1983). As a result, interpersonal relationships tend to be pushed toward instrumental communication with substantial negative expressive meanings. Since the quality of the interaction for school district personnel is instrumental, actual communication tends to be assigned to lower-ranking staff members.

THE HISTORICAL EVOLUTION OF SCHOOL CONSTRUCTION

> In its origins, the school was almost everywhere an unspecific place, without any special facilities. . . . [T]he school building was a community centre for public meetings, celebrations, lectures and even private gatherings. . . . It is only gradually that that function became dominant to the exclusion of the other functions. (Organization for Economic Cooperation and Development, 1978, pp. 12-13)

School buildings did not become objects of interest to architects until the middle of the twentieth century (Castaldi, 1987). The historical development of school buildings can be traced through three periods in history starting with the Hellenistic Era, which lasted from the time of Alexander the Great into the first century B.C. The second part of this era records the development of church grammar schools in Italy, France, Germany, and England during the fifteenth and sixteenth centuries, but the school buildings were not of interest to architects, nor were they designed by them.

The second period was during the early American and post-Civil War era. Castaldi (1987, p. 13) reports that "they were simply shelters in which pupils and teachers might come together." During the post-Civil War period, "the design of the ordinary school building took no account of its nature or various functions. The solution adopted was nothing but an addition of classrooms, one exactly like the others" (Roth, 1966, p. 1 3). The third period began with the twentieth century. During this period, architects became key players in school design, so much so that today's schools are increasingly celebrated as architectural works of art (American Association of School Administrators, 1986).

The first schoolhouse built in the United States in the nineteenth century was adopted from the British model. The schoolhouse measured 50 x 100 feet, and this design remained common in the United States between 1806 to about 1840.

In 1847 the Quincy School, consisting of more than one room, was constructed in the city of Boston. The design was described as the "collection of boxes" or the "egg-crate" arrangement. This plan influenced school design for a century or more.

The second half of the 1800s brought about significant changes in schoolbuildings. Horace Mann and Henry Barnard established the principle of form and function that resulted in specifying buildings as schools. School building was also influenced by Pestalozzi's ideas: (1) education at school is a continuation and extension of parental education; (2) the classroom and school should provide the child with security and intimacy similar to that in the home; and (3) the environment of both the school and home forms a vital part of the child's education (Roth, 1966). The architectural response to his theories of learning was to increase the size of the building and add an auditorium and a Greek Revival or Victorian facade to the Quincy design of elementary schools.

Eveleth (1870) converted Victorian house types into schools. The significance of this activity is that the "house as a school concept is important because the symbolism of the house is mankind's most primitive architectural idea" (no page). Eveleth cited examples by stating that all important civic buildings are founded on the symbolism of the house and most retain the word, such as schoolhouse, courthouse, jailhouse, and firehouse.

In 1873, the addition of kindergarten and secondary schools contributed more changes. The American public high school followed the Kalamazoo Court decision of 1874. This court decision established the right of local school districts to construct and operate high schools at public expense. Cupolas, parapet walls, high ceilings, excessive ornamentation, and central fan heating systems were characteristics of these schools (Leu, 1965).

The first half of the 1900s saw schools grow in number, size, and variety. Frank Lloyd Wright's Hillsdale Home School in Spring Green, Wisconsin, done at the turn of the century, and Dwight Perkins' Carl Schurz High School in Chicago in 1910 were two schools built to relate design to learning theory (see Educational Facilities Laboratories, 1960). By 1917, the federal government was providing substantial support to both vocational and physical education facilities at the secondary school level.

The earliest work in this field, *School Architecture or Contributions to the Improvement of Schoolhouses*, (Barnard, 1848), illustrates the manner by which the study of school facilities has been traditionally reported. Henry Barnard, a specialist in the construction of school buildings, presented his ideas to various groups and eventually wrote each of the presentations down and organized them under two major themes. The first was to present a review of various states' schoolhouses. The second was to present schoolhouse plans as recommended by many educators, including Alcott, Mann, and Emerson. Another standard that was presented was for schools to provide an occasion for the formation of manners, morals, and intellectual attainments (see McClintock and McClintock, 1970, p. 19). Barnard also established that the "schoolhouse was a work of architecture to the degree that the building itself enhanced the school's performance of its cultural task: to be an emblem, for its pupils, of high ethical and rational standards" (McClintock and McClintock, p. 19). A central question in examining schoolhouses during this period was: What would children learn from the schoolhouse itself? The architect, in this case, was to be concerned primarily with the cultural rather than the physical attributes of an edifice.

American Schoolhouses (Dressler, 1911) is the original guide used for building school facilities. This work established the standards for lighting, health, and sanitation. George D. Strayer and N. L. Engelhardt of Teachers College, Columbia, were instrumental in setting up these standards, which were widely adhered to between 1920-1930.

In 1921, Samuel A. Challman of Minnesota, Charles McDermott of New Jersey, and Frank H. Woods of New York met in Atlantic City to discuss the formation of an organization to deal with the issue of school plant planning and construction. From this meeting the National Council on Schoolhouse Construction was founded. The council's purpose was to promote the establishment of standards for school buildings. These standards included expenditure limits, design style, use of space, and safe, healthy conditions. In 1967, the National Council on Schoolhouse Construction changed its name to The Council of Educational Facility Planners, and in 1971 International was added.

In 1927, the California State Legislature requested that the State Department of Education establish a division to monitor school construction within the state. The main arguments for establishing a division of Schoolhouse Planning were: (1) to prevent waste in school construction, (2) to improve the health and safety of pupils, and (3) to make the school facility appropriate for educational needs.

Between 1933 and 1937, the U. S. Government, through the Public Works Administration, became involved in financing school construction. During the 1940s, Europe, Canada, and the United States moved to develop state, federal, and provincial building standards.

Between 1937 and 1947, the California Division of Schoolhouse Planning was associated with many changes in the design of school facilities and in the method of planning and financing them. In 1949, the State of California introduced and implemented a program to allocate state funds to school districts of low financial ability. The program was intended to ensure that every pupil was provided a minimum of classroom space in order to meet his or her educational needs. As stated earlier, the California legislature, upon the first appropriation in 1950, then established a State Allocation Board to control the program and to make the allotments. The Office of Local Assistance was subsequently established.

A change in school design took place during the 1950s, when the "Quincy Box" design was changed to a single-story, rambling school design. This design featured cluster, finger, and campus plans. New construction materials were also used. Glass, concrete, steel, new furnishings, and teaching aids contributed to the changes. Recreational and athletic facilities became standard.

During the 1960s, diversity in school design took place. Open spaces, flexible scheduling, carpeting, air conditioning, movable walls, pods, and team teaching necessitated new designs. Several construction systems emerged. In the 1970s, the changes were prompted by enrollment declines, energy conservation needs, and career education emphasis on community-based school programs. The 1980s focused on ensuring that facilities responded to programmatic needs. Flexible facilities were encouraged to accommodate future programs (see Council of Educational Facility Planners International, 1985; AASA, 1971).

THE SCHOOL STRUCTURE

Generally speaking, school facilities are so expensive that districts limit construction to the minimum facilities required to accommodate immediate student requirements and put off construction as long as possible (Brubaker, 1985). As a result, schools tend to be built without full consideration of educational specifications. District officials respond more readily to enrollment increases than programmatic needs. When building programs are undertaken in response to enrollment pressures rather than to meet programmatic needs, there is a danger that the cultural meaning of the school's physical plant will be lost. When a school plant acquires the culturally significant status of a "school" as distinct from being merely a "building," it becomes an active part of the educational program, serving a "staging function" in support of the learning process (Birch and Johnstone, 1975, p. 14). MacConnell (1957) refers to this symbolic function of the building when reporting that schools have long been considered only as places where school is "kept" and have only recently come to be seen as places that can directly support or inhibit student learning.

When school facilities are built for instructional purposes, they serve as "symbols of community cooperation for the welfare of children and youth" (American Association of School Administrators, 1991, pp. 5, 20; 1971). The structures stand for many years as symbols of the degree to which communities are willing to put their trust and faith in the leadership of educators and policy makers. If rapid enrollment increases or new instructional and building construction technologies create a demand for new school facilities, building programs have to balance long-term community symbolism against immediate design and construction needs (Mills, 1976).

The level of community regard for school buildings can be gauged by whether they are seen as "temples" filled with artifacts of their time or merely as "utility buildings" housing classroom operations (Burlingame, 1984). Burlingame sees contemporary school buildings as cultural statements made by educators and the community, much as Greek statuary and Roman buildings captured the spirit of their own era. As a result, he insists, it is appropriate to compare libraries with gymnasiums or to analyze the characteristics of classroom and laboratory spaces, carpeting, paved parking lots, playgrounds, special offices, and lounges for teachers, in order to ascertain what various eras or communities are expressing about the character and nature of schooling.

Some observers assert that the main function of the school building is the creation of an appealing and supportive environment for learning (Birch and Johnstone, 1975). Beyond capacity and protection from the elements, these observers draw attention to movement, comfort, and aesthetics as factors that influence student and teacher responses. From this perspective, school plans are judged by comfort and excitement as well as cost, ease of maintenance, and safety. Sound architectural designs proclaim school and community identity as well as create pleasant and comfortable spaces for teaching and learning.

The foregoing discussion shows that school facilities have become important architectural objects, invested with substantial community values and meanings. But what evidence is there of actual impact on learning? Taken as a whole, the literature on school structures divides the effects question into three parts:

1. To what extent, if any, do school buildings facilitate or inhibit learning?

2. To the extent that physical facilities have potent effects, do these effects support all educational programs equally, or do various building designs favor particular forms or approaches to education while ignoring or inhibiting others?

3. To the extent that building structures affect learning, does that effect depend on community involvement, trust and respect, or is it a direct consequence of building design, maintenance, and technical sophistication?

EFFECTIVE SCHOOLS AND SCHOOL ENVIRONMENTS

A small group of research studies have examined the overall link between school facilities and educational performance. Evidence from these studies is mixed, though conclusions are often presented as unequivocal.

Smith and his colleagues (Smith and Keith, 1971; Smith et al., 1988), for example, document the process by which a new school facility became neglected and aged and how this change affected the performance of faculty, staff, and students. Two separate studies reporting on the same facility fifteen years apart report a strong linkage between performance and school facility quality. From this work one is reminded of Churchill's quote, "We shape our buildings, but thereafter they shape us" (Leu, 1965, p. 95).

By contrast, Phi Delta Kappa (1980) shows how the process by which school buildings are prepared for students and staff may differ qualitatively. This report, however, finds no evidence that the physical plant characteristics are associated with outcome measures. In the West Vigo Elementary School case, for example, the negative aspects of the process were (1) limited community and staff involvement; (2) controversy over the choice of building style by the educational staff; (3) the move into the building with no preplanning by staff, teachers, and students; and (4) controversy over the designation and selection of a principal just two weeks before the move. In contrast, the same study describes a positive process in the case of the Mary W. French Elementary School. In that case, the voters approved the issuance of bonds for upgrading the quality of the district's school buildings. The upgrading included new construction, reconstruction, and the closing and/or razing of several existing schools. The parents believed the decision to renovate French School was symbolically significant. The staff involved in the move described it as cooperative and collaborative. They also perceived the school as a warm, friendly building. The parents and faculty were pleased that the architects retained the integrity of the school by preserving the old ceilings and other special effects.

Miskel and Ogawa (1988) review this part of the school effects literature within the larger context of works dealing with "organizational ecology." This term is not commonly used to discuss school issues, but is useful in linking facility research with the broader issues of school climate and ethos (see Taguiri, 1968).

A few studies have reported on the link between school ecological elements and educational outcomes. The findings are diverse. Three studies (Weber, 1971; Rutter et al., 1979; and the 1980 Phi Delta Kappa study cited above) find no significant link between physical facilities and student performance. Weber studied the relationship between the age of four traditional "egg-crate" school buildings and reading achievement among inner-city children. Within this narrow band of variation, he concluded that successful schools do not require outstanding physical facilities. This study is of limited value, however, because of the similarity in design and age of the buildings studied.

Rutter et al. (1979) tested the impact of building age (ranging from ten to over a hundred years old), decoration, and upkeep on student achievement, attendance, behavior, and delinquency. They found little difference in school impact except for split-site schools, which did seem to have better results with student behavior and delinquency. The effect of split-site schools with buildings dispersed and closer to the clientele may be more responsive to local cultures and student values.

Four studies report a positive link between facility conditions and student learning. McGuffey (1982), comparing the Quincy Grammar school constructed in Boston in 1848 to other modern schools, showed that building age has a statistically significant impact on school achievement (p. 274). Attitude and behavior differences were significant in favor of the newly modernized buildings. His two general conclusions were that (1) obsolete and inadequate school facilities detract from the learning process, whereas modern, controlled physical environments enhance it; and (2) facilities may have a differential impact on the performance of pupils in different grades and for different subjects (p. 276). Plumley (1978) reported similar findings in an earlier study. There was a significant inverse relationship between student achievement and the age of the nonmodernized buildings.

A survey study reported by Karst (1984) asked teachers and pupils to rank school facilities from superior to inferior. He found that as quality declines, the differences between teachers in the good facilities' and teachers in the poor facilities' perceptions increase. Pupils varied significantly in their user attitudes as building quality declined. Pupils were more likely to evaluate their schools as the researchers did than were teachers. Hawkins and Overbaugh (1988) conducted a comparative study of American and Japanese schools. They found that when the school building is a reflection of the community, increased learning will take place. The facility needs to accommodate a variety of individual learning styles. The school building aids learning when it readily meets the user's needs. The interface between facility and learning occurs when communication is fostered.

Bowers and Burkett (1988) report their findings of a comparative study looking at a modern school building and an older school building. The students in the modern building scored significantly higher in reading, listening, language, and arithmetic than did students in the older structure. Students in the modern facility were disciplined significantly less frequently, had a significantly higher attendance record, and were in better health than students in the older building.

Some additional evidence of facility impact comes from school-climate research. Reviews of this research indicate that physical facility size is the characteristic most likely to affect schooling (Anderson, 1982; Duke and Perry, 1978; Flagg, 1964; Miskel and Ogawa, 1988; Morocco, 1978; New York State Department of Education, 1976; Sinclair, 1970). Smaller schools are more effective in improving behavior, attendance, and performance, and school appearance is more important than the age of the building in terms of student impact.

Some studies, such as the one conducted by Lezotte and Passalcqua (1982), are not clear in their reference to school buildings. Their descriptors of school buildings appear to include school personnel, equipment, and materials rather than the physical facility. Lezotte and Passalcqua write that their findings show that the "school building accounts for significant variance in achievement beyond the influence of prior achievement" (p. 292). Because they are unclear on their term "school building," a review of studies like the above are not included in this report.

While not based on social science research, a West Virginia legal case supports the view that school facility conditions impact substantially on educational quality. In *Pauley v. Bailey* (1982, 1984) the court found that adequate facilities are necessary for a thorough and efficient system of education. Because the condition of facilities in West Virginia ranged from deplorable to exemplary, the judge ordered that a master plan be developed that would incorporate the standards for a thorough and efficient system of education into all phases of the educational system, including facilities. The master plan was to contain, among other criteria, school facility standards that would guarantee high-quality facilities to complement the type of educational system called for by the state constitution (see Truby, 1983; *Pauley v. Bailey*, 1982; *Pauley v. Bailey*, 1984).

THE PROCESS OF CONSTRUCTING NEW SCHOOLS

While a historical review of developments in research and scholarly analysis of school facilities construction helps put this complex and generally unsophisticated literature into one useful perspective, it is also useful to examine it in relation to the processes involved in planning, constructing, and utilizing school facilities. The remainder of this report summarizes insights gleaned from published reports and scholarly works related to each phase in this process.

School designs, as noted by Birch and Johnstone (1975), link instructional processes with physical space. To successfully make this linkage, planning activities must cover a broad range of technical and educational considerations, ranging from instructional program design through building construction procedures to evaluation of completed facilities (Earthman, 1986).

In most school districts a "facility planner" is formally designated and assigned the responsibility of organizing the planning process (Strevell and Burke, 1959; Castaldi, 1987). The role and status of these persons are directly related to school district size (Kowalski, 1989; Abramson, 1981; Carter and Rosenbloom, 1989; Davis and Loveless, 1981). The larger the district, the higher the position and status within the organization. It is further demonstrated that the complexity of the process requires additional administrative skills and leadership. Their tasks are to organize faculty, professional personnel, administrators, nonprofessional personnel, and students into two basic planning groups. The first is the executive planning team, which has the full authority to develop the plans necessary for building the school. This team consists of the chief school administrator, an administrative assistant, the architect, an educational consultant, a faculty member, a legal advisor, and other school officials such as school board members. The executive planning team reviews all aspects of the design. Since the team's duty is to ensure that educational specifications are appropriately integrated into the design of the structure, educational consultants generally play a prominent role on this committee.

The second planning group organized by the facilities planner is the institutional planning team. This team usually consists of fifteen members from a cross-section of professional and nonprofessional staff. The team's task is to review educational specifications and all architectural plans. It submits reactions and recommendations to the executive planning team as well as serves as a liaison group between the executive planning team, faculty, students, and interested parents (See Castaldi, 1987).

The purpose of including community members in the planning and development of an educational facility is two-fold: the district wishes to construct a facility that meets the community's needs and at the same time wishes to encourage future citizen involvement in the activities of the facility after it is completed (MacKenzie, 1989, p. 29; MacConnell, 1957). The involvement of citizens has three effects: (1) it helps the planning committee discover many more community needs; (2) it convinces citizens that the facility is for everyone; and (3) it builds credibility between the planners of the facility and the people that facility is designed to serve. A report by the American Association of School Administrators (1971) suggests that a district may encourage community involvement through a process they call "charrette." Charrette is a

> free-flowing, open-ended conclave structured to facilitate communication and expedite decision-making. An educational charrette is a technique for studying and resolving educational facility development problems within the context of total community planning needs. Professionals and concerned parents listen to one another; students and teachers tell what they like, want, or do not want; architects and city planners talk with PTA leaders; tax payers whose prime concern is cost-cutting have their say; and interested community members express their concerns. (p. 29)

Professionals involved in the institutional planning team typically include an architect, several types of engineers, and other specialists.

Without making a distinction between the professional and executive functions, Jenkins (1985) identifies the work of the educational planner with activities that fit into Kaufman's (1956) concept of executive action: preparation of a master plan for both design and capital fundraising, drawing up educational specifications, incorporation of these specifications into the building program, providing for project coordination, assuring proper orientation of critical groups and individuals, and undertaking the postoccupancy evaluation (see California State Department of Education, 1986b, for a similar specification of tasks).

A STEP-BY-STEP REVIEW OF SCHOOL CONSTRUCTION PROCESSES

As noted in the theoretical framework section of this report the process of school facility construction is appropriately divided into nine distinctive phases or steps. A review of what the literature has to say about the content and procedures used by school districts during each of these steps is presented next. Each step is summarized in terms of the characteristic activities required as well as the roles played by executive leadership, professional expertise, and political representative agents in guiding the conduct of these activities.

STEP ONE: NEEDS ASSESSMENT

The first step in the construction of new schools is needs assessment. According to Boles (1969), this is the "getting organized" stage in the construction process. Some general activities performed at this stage include defining the educational problem, analyzing the problem areas, conceptualizing and designing the plan, evaluating the plan, specifying the plan, implementing the plan, and finally obtaining feedback about the plan (Earthman, 1986; The Council of Educational Facility Planners International, 1985; Hertz and Day, 1987; Hill, 1986; MacKenzie, 1989). Procedural decisions must be considered, such as how decisions will be made, who will be involved, and when discussions will take place. The district's educational philosophy is usually used to justify requests to formulate long-range goals.

Critical actors who must receive verification of the need for a new school facility include the board of education, community representatives, the superintendent, regional and state educational officials, and others. Since many individuals are involved in the construction process, it is important to establish clear communication patterns. Agencies and offices at local, regional, and state levels need to be coordinated and kept informed. Maintaining an updated list of participants and their roles is an important activity. A task outline should be developed with established goals and deadlines.

Planning resources, personnel, and funds are required to conduct the "getting organized" phase. Usually the planning agents for the school district are the board of education, the administrator, and the district staff. District administrative personnel include persons such as educator-planners, program specialists, library specialists, operations and maintenance superintendents, business administrators and financial analysts. The school site personnel are principals, teachers, other administrators, instructional staff, support staff, students, PTA and advisory committees, and the community. General educational resources include professional associations; educational consultants; regional, state, and provincial education agencies; universities; colleges; and research agencies and institutions.

The technical and legal personnel include architects, engineers, legal counsel, assessment and land agencies, construction managers, contractors, equipment and furniture suppliers, and other technical specialists. The community planning personnel include local planning offices, commissions, and departments; regional planning agencies and commissions; civic departments; local resource bureaus; residential development resources; planning and development consultants; and other local resources. Additional resources reside in the federal agencies and departments, state and provincial departments, national and international professional associations, and international agencies, all of which provide a variety of information and assistance.

Throughout the needs assessment step, the executive function, usually discharged through the facility planner, involves initiating organizational response to information reaching the district regarding demographic changes, student enrollment increases, and community growth. The professional expertise needed at this stage is primarily concerned with demographic analysis. This expertise, brought by a consulting demographer, a city manager, or school staff member, alerts the facility planner to enrollment increases or new housing development permits that were requested and approved. The representative function needed at this stage involves formal recognition of facility needs and the approval of planning resources, such as payment for the services of a consulting demographer. Another instance of representative leadership arises when parents inquire about school facilities for their children.

Executive, professional, and representative functions can emerge strongly or weakly, and may occur in any order. In some instances, one or more functions may be neglected entirely. Before the planning and organizing for the construction of a new school can begin, however, some executive must act. That is, at this stage the executive function is defined by initiative, stimulating organizational response to community change.

These core functions are sometimes contested. The executive, for example, may be preoccupied with other matters, or may not wish to act on information regarding demographic changes and enrollment increases. If this happens, a representative group (such as a minority community member) may enter the process to force the school district to consider building new schools. Professional leadership may dominate the process when, for example, a survey of population changes leads a staff expert to initiate consideration of facility needs. In these special cases community representatives or staff experts take over executive responsibilities, frequently producing confusion or conflict in the school organization.

STEP TWO: LONG-RANGE PLANNING

The second step in the construction of new schools is long-range planning. A long-range plan takes into account projected growth, limited financial resources, community-based school utilization studies, and recent legislative action (see Blair, 1987, p. 2; Hill, 1987; Lows, 1987). Castaldi (1987), Jenkins (1985), and others (Blair, 1987; California State Department of Education, 1986b; Council of Educational Facility Planners, International, 1985; Day, 1984; Day and Speicher, 1985; Eismann, 1976; Engelhardt, 1970; Leu, 1965; Earthman, 1986) have identified specific tasks required for the development of a long-range plan. The first task is to make an enrollment projection. Information on specific residential tracks is extremely useful in selecting sites for new school buildings and in determining future costs of student transportation. The next task is to conduct a building survey covering assessment of the adequacy of existing facilities, calculation of building capacities, and identification of unmet educational needs. From this survey a long-range building plan is prepared for submittal to the school board. Finally, representatives from the community participate in the process by expressing their desires. According to most authorities, the best examples of long-range planning are developed by the joint efforts of the community and the school district (California State Department of Education, 1986b; Keough and Earthman, 1984; Williams, 1983). As they are completed, new facilities are evaluated and an update of the facilities master plan is prepared (Graves, 1984a, 1984b; Blair, 1987).

During the long-range planning stage, the executive function is dominated by the need to organize the complex planning process. It is the executive who determines the time frame for planning; typically a three-, five-, or ten-year time frame is chosen. The executive also calls on specialists and groups needed to provide information and support services for the planning process. The executive leads the process, makes decisions regarding form and procedure, and brings closure to the process.

The professional function enters the long-range planning process on an advisory basis. School site administrators may be called upon to provide information regarding the current condition of their schools and whether or not they can absorb the new growth. Certified and classified staff may also be called upon to provide information on current changes in educational technology and methodology and building needs that may have an impact on future facility design.

The representative function enters the process by providing legitimacy and direction for the planning process. The school board acknowledges and supports the planning process by reviewing procedures, integrating competing community-group demands, and providing formal authority and fiscal support for the planning effort.

Contested control over the long-range planning process often arises when the technical judgments of professional staffers are advanced as finished plans (as when a city manager publishes a five-year plan specifying future school sites and size and design of the structures without first consulting the school district personnel and/or board members). A contest over control may also emerge from representative groups, such as the school board, if planning conclusions are adopted on the basis of interest-group priorities rather than executive rationality or expert advise. What is necessary to prevent contestation during this step is to have representatives from all three core functions participate, limiting their activities to their roles, in order to ensure that the long-range plan focuses on the school district's needs and aims.

STEP THREE: FISCAL PLANNING

The third step in the construction of new schools is the development of a fiscal plan derived from the district's capital improvement plan and budget. At this stage the method for funding and financing schools needs to be determined. Sometimes school districts hire financial advisors to provide these services. (See Wood, 1986; Alexander and Wood, 1983). These financial advisors consult with architects, engineers, and bond attorneys in the preparation of a financing plan. However, most school districts rely on their administrative staff to determine which sort of financing they qualify for and which is the most appropriate for them to pursue.

School districts have available to them four types of fund sources which may be used for the construction of new schools: (1) state grants and loans; (2) local taxation options; (3) leasing programs; and (4) asset management. Each one of these sources has its advantages and disadvantages and school districts benefit from them differentially. Tapping into the specific source requires interaction with different state and local agencies. In California, the two state agencies that approve all construction regardless of financing are the Office of the State Architect and the California State Department of Education/School Facility Planning Division. The State Allocation Board and the Office of Local Assistance deal with the state's lease-purchase-agreement school construction funding program. The California School Finance Authority aids when districts seek tax-exempt bonds for financing their school construction.

State grants and loans

Although there are no federal funds available for school building, there are state funds available. These funds are available in the form of grants or loans. The state of California acquires funds from three sources:

1. School district "excess" repayments, the amount by which school district principal and interest payments on State School Building Aid loans exceed debt service requirements for state school construction bonds
2. Tidelands oil revenues, an amount of $150 million appropriated annually through 1988-89, used principally for new school construction
3. Proceeds from State of California bond sales, the amount authorized by voters to raise state funds for school facilities by approving the Lease-Purchase Bonds Acts of 1982 and 1984.

From the three sources of funds, California reallocates moneys to the school districts through the LeRoy Greene Lease-Purchase Agreement, which is the most common form of school facility construction funding in the state. Additionally, the California School Finance Authority was created in 1985 by the legislature to provide alternative assistance in school housing. The Authority's purpose is to reconstruct, remodel, or replace existing school buildings that are educationally inadequate or that do not meet current structural safety requirements. It may also acquire new school sites and buildings to be made available to school districts for the pupils of the public school system. Finally, it has the responsibility of assisting school districts by providing access to financing for working capital and capital improvements. The Authority is comprised of the State Treasurer (designated as Chair), the director of the State Department of Finance, and the Superintendent of Public Instruction (see Graves, 1983).

School districts may use a variety of means for raising revenue and for acquiring funds to construct school facilities. Some districts may use current revenue or "pay-as-you-go" financing. This method is usually available to wealthy and large school districts. Some districts are able to set aside each year money to be used in the future. These funds are called "sinking funds," which the school district subsequently uses to construct the building. This method of financing school construction is not legal in every state (Ambrosie, 1983; Augenblick, 1984; King and Kimbrough, 1982). Some school districts, such as those in Hawaii, receive all of their support for facility construction from the state (Thompson, 1988). Others, such as those in California and Florida, receive the major portion of their support from the state. Maryland's school districts are having their dependence on state support for facility construction reduced.

States' school finance formulas differ with respect to support for facility construction. In Arizona, for example, both capital outlay costs and debt service obligations are included in the state's equalization formula. What this means is that less wealthy districts receive higher levels of state aid for school construction, resulting in increased state control over the process of planning and constructing schools (Jordan, 1988). In contrast, Nebraska's financing of school construction is totally a local school district responsibility. Permissive legislation and regulation form the basis for the state and school district interrelationship (Hudson, 1988).

Other methods that states employ to finance the construction of school facilities from the state level include flat grants, equalization aid, state loans, authorities, and lease-rental financing. School districts most often fund their school construction locally through general obligation bonds. Well over 75 percent of all capital outlay costs are in general obligation bonds (Gipson, 1985; Hansen, 1984; Cambron-McCabe, 1984; California Coalition for Fair School Finance, 1984; Chick, 1987; Education Writers Association, 1989).

Local taxation options

General obligation bonds. General obligation bonds (GOBs) may be issued by a school district when there is a lack of cash flow or resources to tax. The district issues bonds where payment is guaranteed by the full faith and credit of the issuer. These bonds receive federal tax-exempt status on their interest earnings. Nearly all school bonds are serial bonds, numbered and payable semiannually or annually during the life of the issue. The other type of bonds are term bonds, which mature on the same date and are redeemed at the same time. Four major criteria are used to develop bond ratings for school districts. The debt burden of the district, administrative factors such as growth or decline in the school system, tax assessment burden, and the general state of the economy of the area all serve to establish bond ratings for school districts (see Education Writers Association, 1989, p. 31).

Since general obligation bonds have to be approved by the electorate, some researchers have sought to determine when citizens are likely to support taxation such as GOBs. Bell and Coombs (1987) identified three necessary conditions for a citizen's yes vote on a school-tax increase: (1) citizens must perceive that the school system needs the requested money; (2) citizens must believe that the money will be well spent; and (3) citizens must believe that the higher taxes are bearable.

Their study showed that citizens who are parents of children in public schools are more likely to believe schools need more money.

Castaldi (1987) presents a strategy for developing community support. The strategy calls for determining the level of current public support for a potential bond referendum and selecting a propaganda technique that is motivating and in harmony with public sentiment. Castaldi advises a citizen's advisory committee be established. Most authorities (Castaldi, 1987; California Coalition for Fair School Finance, 1984; Chang and Albiani, 1987) believe it is better to start the public information program early in order to provide the citizenry sufficient and comprehensive information.

The Education Writers Association (1989) reported that bond approval rates are increasing slightly, from 76.6 percent in 1986 to 79.8 percent in 1988. Several changes in GOBs, which tend towards benefit for individuals rather than banks, are reported. First, the 1986 tax-reform law specifies bonds are tax-free to individuals but may not be advantageous to corporations. Second, banks are reducing their investments in bonds. And third, bonds are more costly if marketed to individuals rather than to banks.

Developer fees. Many school districts levy developer fees directly on new construction. All or any part of the fees imposed by the district on new construction may be used for new permanent school facilities. School districts require developers to show evidence that such fees have been paid before building permits can be issued by the responsible local government agency. School districts can assess developer fees on new housing and commercial or industrial development unless and until the governing board has made the finding that a dedication bears a reasonable relationship to the needs of the community for elementary or high school facilities and is reasonably related and limited to the needs caused by the development (see Kirschenstein, 1980; Smit and Hesse-Wallace, 1980). The fees are limited to a certain amount per square foot for residential construction and a lesser amount per square foot for commercial and industrial construction.

201 developer fees. When temporary housing for students is sought, the 201 developer fees may be applicable in one of three forms: fees levied by the city, the county or by both. These fees may be required as a condition for approval of residential development.

Special taxes. Cities, counties, and special districts, by a two-thirds vote of qualified electors, may impose special taxes. Sometimes school districts benefit from tax bond sale alternatives, which generally combine the functions of creating the revenue source and leveraging that source through the sale of bonds. Revenue may be generated through the creation of "benefit" or "special" assessment districts. The "Poway" Plan, for example, allows a district to lease school facilities from a non-profit corporation. The non-profit corporation sells bonds to finance the construction of the facilities. The district collects money to pay the lease through an assessment levied on properties benefitting from the proposed construction. Under this plan, all landowners in the proposed assessment district must consent to the assessment before it can be implemented.

Anticipation notes. Another method of raising the capital for near-term capital needs is the issuance of tax and revenue anticipation notes. This involves issuing one-year notes and using the invested proceeds to cover short-term cash-flow deficits and/or to produce additional revenue. A school district can issue and sell tax and revenue anticipation notes either by competitive sale or as a negotiated sale with an underwriter or bank. The funds are invested until needed to finance the project for which they were designed, and the notes are redeemed by the anticipated revenue when it is received.

Mello-Roos. The Mello-Roos Community Facilities Act is a form of municipal financing. The structure is set up so that the local government and its constituency not only control the development approval process but the financing process as well. The Mello-Roos Act authorizes a Community Facilities District (CFD) where there are twelve or more voters within the district. When there are fewer than twelve registered voters living within the district, authorization requires qualified electors, owners of the land within the district (Drexel, Burnham & Lambert, 1989, p. 1).

Lease-purchase agreements

Leasing has been used by school districts for a number of years to lease and ultimately acquire relocatable classroom units. Lease-type financing has several titles: municipal lease financing, installment purchase financing, or lease-purchase financing. All are based on a lease agreement. Lease agreements are available to school districts to make payments to a lessor for use of equipment (i.e., relocatable classroom units). The leases are usually sold by an underwriter (a bank) to investors, and the proceeds are used by the district to acquire the equipment. This method can also be used to finance capital outlay. Lease agreements are not a source of revenue but rather a method of leveraging a revenue source in order to construct or otherwise obtain a capital facility needed by the school district. The security for the transaction is the asset that is financed. Not until all lease payments have been made does title pass to the school district.

Municipal leasing. Municipal leasing has some significant advantages. This type of leasing is not considered long-term; therefore, a public entity's debt limitation will not be affected. Implementing fees are not added to the amount being financed. Also, voter approval is not required. The district or lessee retains complete control over the design, acquisition or construction, and management of whatever is financed. Title to the capital equipment is held by the lessor to secure the financing.

LeRoy Greene Purchase-Agreement. As mentioned earlier, California school districts tend to finance their school facilities through a LeRoy Greene Lease-Purchase Agreement. The school system enters into a lease-purchase agreement with another entity, such as the state, duly powered to act as lessor. An investment bank purchases the obligation from the issuer and sells them to investors. The technique has the advantage of not adding to the issuer's bonded debt capacity. The reason for this is that lease-purchase payments are appropriated annually, and are thus deemed as current expense of the issue, not bonded indebtedness (Pierce, 1989, p. 50).

A lease-purchase agreement binds the district and the state to comply with all conditions stipulated in the original document and to any special conditions agreed upon in all subsequent amendments. The various provisions are collectively referred to as "the project." The lease-purchase agreement is binding once SAB approves the project. SAB has full charge of acquisition, construction, and completion of all projects. This control is exercised by approving applications for lease-purchase projects, making apportionments of school building funds, and establishing regulations, policies, and procedures.

The process of entering into a lease-purchase agreement begins when the school district submits an application requesting funds for building new schools. This application is submitted to the regional Office of Local Assistance. A separate application by the school district is required for each project. Each application is assigned a project number. A relationship is established with the OLA to complete the first six fundamental steps in the construction process. All steps completed are then verified through regulatory forms. The conduct of the construction of new schools under this plan is thus regulated and standardized throughout.

California, at the present time, has a school-facilities package that allows more school districts to qualify for state funding; however, school districts are required to match any state funding dollar for dollar with local resources.

Certificates of participation. Certificates of participation (COPs) are similar to a lease-purchase by a district. This method of funding is an outgrowth of the traditional lease-purchasing financing. COPs integrate the benefits of capital leasing programs with those of tax-exempt bonds, which attract investors and yield lower interest costs. Specifically, COPs are certificates that represent an undivided percentage interest in lease payments made by the school district to a lessor for the lease of equipment and/or capital projects. The certificates are sold by an underwriter to investors and the proceeds are used by the district to acquire or construct such projects.

Asset management

Another financial procedure that may be used by school districts to acquire funds is asset management. Asset management is a broad term that encompasses several methods of utilizing capital assets and property already owned to acquire additional capital facilities. Some methods are sale of property, lease of property, tax-increment financing (redevelopment agency), and joint venturing.

Sale of property. The sale of property to generate funds for school building may be necessary for several reasons: zoning, condition, and size of the site; condition or disposition of any building on the site; street access to the parcel; and utility hookups. School districts sometimes lease out property to generate revenue for capital outlay or other purposes.

Tax increment. Tax-increment financing or redevelopment is another way to finance capital outlay. Tax increment comes from the growth in property-tax revenue within the redevelopment project area. The redevelopment causes an increase in the value of the property in the affected area and, therefore, the tax on that property increases. This additional tax increment revenue is then used to finance the redevelopment project, which may include a school.

Joint venturing. Joint venturing is a combination of all of the above: sale, leasing, nonprofit corporation, and redevelopment agency status.

Properly used, the private/public joint venture concept, when originated by the school district in conformance with state goals and objectives, can become a viable alternative source of revenue for California school districts.

During the fiscal planning process the executive function is primarily a matter of decision-making. Determination of what resources will be used in the construction of the new school is made at this step. Professionalism enters at this stage to provide technical assistance in meeting legal requirements and identifying sources of funds. The representative function enters this stage in order to mobilize support for needed resource allocation. The school board, in its representative role, decides whether and how much debt to incur for the construction needs. If the district plans to obtain funds through a general obligation bond, it is necessary for the community to be informed and supportive. Representatives can be used as positive spokespersons for the district. In order to increase the likelihood of parent and community support for funds for the construction of schools, the executive assumes the leadership in organizing these groups and in providing required information to the representative function. While final approval is a representative matter, executives generally assume the leadership in organizing parent and community support groups. Figures 3 and 4 illustrate the types of financing and state agency involvement.

STEP FOUR: EDUCATIONAL SPECIFICATIONS DEVELOPMENT, SITE SELECTION, AND BUILDING DESIGN

The fourth step, the school building planning, includes three distinct tasks: (1) developing educational specifications, (2) planning and selecting the site, and (3) designing the building. Often these tasks are treated as separate steps in the facility construction process, but there is a real danger in allowing these tasks to become separated. The literature shows many examples of the conflicts that can arise if these three tasks are not properly integrated (see for example, Day, 1985a, 1985b, 1985c, 1983b; Day and Speicher, 1985).

Educational specifications

Practitioners are advised to remember that "form can follow function in school structures only if the functions are presented in an understandable way to the architect" (Mayfield, 1984). This defines the first key task of the fourth step in the building construction process. School building functions must be explicated in detail if architects are to per-

FIGURE 3
School Districts' School Construction Funds Sources

State Grants and Loans	*Local Taxation Options*	*Leasing Agreements*	*Asset Management*
Flat Grants	General Obligation Bonds	LeRoy Greene Lease-Purchase Agreement	Sale of Property
Equalization Aid	Developer Fees	Municipal Lease Financing	Lease of Property
State Loans	201 Developer Fees	Installment Purchase Financing	Tax-increment Financing (Redevelopment)
Authorities	Assessment "Poway" Plan	Lease-Purchase Financing	Joint Venturing
Lease Rentals	Tax and Revenue Anticipation Notes	Certificates of Participation	
	Mello-Roos		

form their design tasks appropriately. This detailing of building functions is identified in the school facilities literature as the development of "educational specifications." Educational specifications are used by the architect to develop the architectural specifications for the school (Day, 1985a, 1985b, 1985c, 1983b; Everett, 1986).

Even though McQuaid's (1958) work is from the fifties, his observations sum up the critical aspects of combining the educational specifications development, building design, and site selection tasks. He wrote, "there is no such thing as a temporary school—and therefore, no escape from a long, discerning look into the educational future" (p. 39). He explains further that public schools have changed twice in the last two hundred years. The first change was to move from one-room schoolhouses into multiroom buildings. The second change was to add "program space" to the "classroom space" (p. 82) (see Manning, 1967; and Seaborne, 1971).

In California, the Department of General Services, under the police

FIGURE 4
School Financing State Agency Involvement

State Grants and Loans	Local Taxation Options	Leasing Agreements	Asset Management
California School Finance Authority (CSFA)	California School Finance Authority	State Allocation Board (SAB)	California School Finance Authority
Office of the State Architect (OSA)	Office of the State Architect	Office of the State Architect	Office of the State Architect
California State Department of Education/School Facility Planning Division (SDE/SFPD)	California State Department of Education/School Facility Planning Division	California State Department of Education/School Facility Planning Division	California State Department of Education/School Facility Planning Division
		Office of Local Assistance (OLA)	

power of the state, supervises the design and construction of any capital improvement in excess cost of $20,000. No school district is authorized to construct or reconstruct any school building, regardless of the source of funding, unless and until one of the following criteria has been met: (1) the district architect certifies that the project satisfies the construction cost and allowable area standards, and (2) the district agrees that in subsequent applications for state funding for school construction, construction not certified will be deducted from allowable building area (see Holt, 1987).

The architecture of the school has a bearing on the cost of a school. Knirk (1979) identified several cost categories: surveys and consultants, 1 percent; bonding, 1 percent; site costs, 10 percent; landscaping and development, 7 percent; architects and engineers, 7 percent; heating and cooling, 6-11 percent; plumbing 4-6 percent; electrical, 3-8 percent; equipment and moveable furnishings, 7 percent; and miscellaneous, 2 percent. The remaining 40 percent is applied to the physical construction of the facility.

Floor plans. The same researcher identified eight sample floor plans normally used to build schools: corridor, courtyard, finger, loft, circular, cluster, campus, and open. The corridor plan is a rectangular plan with classrooms on either side of a corridor. The courtyard and finger plans are variations of the corridor plan. These two plans are not desirable if the building is to be air conditioned. The extensive surface area of the exterior walls also increases the cost of the building. The loft plan offers a large amount of open space, which can be arranged and rearranged with relative ease. This plan is ideal for air conditioning, but noise and odors are more difficult to control. The circular plan is another open design which is internally flexible. This building is usually a single story building. The cluster school is ideally suited to acoustical or odor problems. The clusters may vary in size and shape but expansion is not as readily possible. Another design, the campus plan, is a macrodesign; it may incorporate the corridor, finger, loft and circular designs. This design is essentially a series of schools on a single plot of land.

Gump (1980), in his analysis of school design in the seventies, wrote that the forces for the new open design in the United States, Great Britain, and Australia came from three directions. The first was grounded in an educational rationale which maintained that unpartitioned space was necessary for the open educational programs being developed. This notion was heavily influenced by the British infant schools. The second force pressing for construction of open schools came from the architectural profession. The new designs enabled architects to import imagination and originality in an area previously highly restricted. The third force was that the basic building cost was substantially less than the traditional design. This third force was particularly potent in the beginning phases of the era.

Landscaping. Other researchers (Lindley, 1985) have had a concern with landscaping as part of the schoolhouse design. These researchers believe that the schoolhouse is the largest residence in the community and should be a good neighbor by exhibiting attractive and functional landscaping. The belief that site planning is the act of arranging the external physical environment to support human behavior is common among these writers. Attractive landscaping is based on the assumption that the external physical setting surrounding a school facility contributes to learning, enjoyment, and pride. Frederick et al.'s (1976) notion that physical settings have some amount of control over how people behave in them is instructive. Certain structures impede personal contact within the setting, whereas others communicate the architect's intention that interaction should take place among people within that building.

Site selection

Selecting the school site is a major task requiring executive leadership. Site selection involves three tasks: (1) applying selection criteria to each prospective site; (2) approving the selection by the board of education; and (3) developing criteria to govern the selection of a site. In California, the State Department of Education/School Facility Planning Division reviews and approves all new school sites and additions to school sites regardless of the source of funding (California State Department of Education, 1987, p. 2).

The site specifications that need to be considered and understood by those affected include land area needed for buildings, entrance areas, landscaped areas, parking, bus loading, driveways, services, playfields and other physical education facilities, community facilities, special requirements for stormwater retention ponds, sewage treatment plan, easement for utilities, and natural wooded or wetland areas. Other considerations in site selection and development are traffic and access, utility needs, soils needs, views, community visibility, image, future expansion, future adaptability, reuse potential, zoning, building codes, regulation restrictions, security, police and fire protection, and linkage to and joint use of other community facilities (see Brubaker, 1986; Council of Educational Facility Planners, International, 1985; Engelhardt, 1970; Hill, 1984; Tanner, 1985).

Mechanical engineering advice may be sought regarding availability of utilities, building orientation, and the type of construction necessary (MacConnell, 1957). Civil engineering assistance is used to secure property descriptions and land titles, interpret title reports, and determine the availability of utilities and storm drainage as well as the accessibility of the school to its neighborhood and the limitations imposed on the site development by its topographical conditions. A foundation engineer may be used to analyze the physical properties of the soil in relation to the construction of the buildings. Lastly, an acoustical engineer may be needed to reduce the effects of noise.

If the site is within two miles of an airport, the California State Department of Education/School Facility Planning Division may request an investigation by the Division of Aeronautics, a map of the site and its location relative to the airport. The investigation by the

Division of Aeronautics would determine noise level, safety, and landing patterns. After aeronautics has completed its study, CSDE/SFPD notifies the district to proceed or not.

A field visit with the CSDE/SFPD consultant is necessary. If the site is to be purchased by the state, the consultant needs to have three acceptable sites for comparison purposes. The CSDE/SFPD consultant evaluates the three sites using the Field Site Review Form. The district, then, obtains authorization to proceed with site appraisals.

Building design and selection of the architect

A third key task to be accomplished during this step, building design, is usually assumed by the architect. Selection of the architect is an important decision made with great care. Frank Lloyd Wright once said, "A doctor can bury his mistakes but an architect can only advise his client to plant vines" (Knirk, 1979, p. vii).

The main reason for constructing schools is to provide favorable, productive conditions for learning. The curriculum determines the activities and programs to be housed in the school. The physical size and learning shape of the classroom, learning center, instructional resources room, and library have a direct effect on the activities that go on within each of those areas. There is no better time for implementing a curriculum change than when constructing new or remodeling old facilities.

Kutkat (1983), an educator, explains the advantage of selecting the architect right after the school board determined it had a need for school buildings. The district found that having the architect participate in planning activities enabled them to build cost-effective schools. Wright (1983) likewise hired an architect and a capital expenditure manager to work as a team in order to implement several cost-saving measures.

To insure that the proposed building results in a school, educational specialists and community representatives should be in direct and continuing contact with the architect. First, educational specialists assure that ideas about the general character and design of the school are exchanged. Second, they help the architect arrange the school so that parents and other patrons can be a part of it. Third, they provide direct input about community activities that need to be accommodated in school buildings. And fourth, they serve as another channel for the community to communicate their desires during a time when a significant educational move is being made that will affect everyone

(Brubaker, 1982, 1985, 1988; Cold, 1986; Day, 1983a; Elhanini, 1986; Hedley and Brokaw, 1984).

The educational specification development, site selection, and building design step has several junctures at which the professional and representative functions can easily come into conflict with the executive. For example, in the selection of a site, political considerations may override educational ones, granting the representative function dominance. The architect may assume the leadership in regards to the design of the facility so that the wishes of the community and the needs of the educational personnel are ignored. In this case, the facility may be architecturally sound but may not be an effective learning environment. It falls to the executive to insure that the district benefits from professional services and representative support while keeping the design process moving toward conclusion.

STEP FIVE: BIDDING AND CONTRACTING

Once the school design has been approved and the site selected, the school district places the project up for bid. Five tasks are involved in the bidding process: (1) locating bidders, (2) issuing and retrieving documents, (3) receiving and tabulating bids, (4) analyzing the bids, and (5) awarding the bids (see Chan, 1983).

Earthman (1986) identified three contractual agreements: (1) single contract with a lump sum, (2) construction management, and (3) design-and-build contract. The most frequent approach is to let a single-sum contract to a general contractor. However, it is sometimes advantageous for school districts to consider multiple contracts with firms specializing in specific tasks (Kutkat, 1983; Haun and Earthman, 1983; Herron, 1983).

The usual procedure is to review the complete architectural plans and specifications at a pre-bid conference between the architect and potential contractors. Following a closely monitored bidding process, the contract is awarded. Bidding and contracting are not well covered in the literature. The technical nature of the step serves to emphasize the legal aspect; almost no attention is given to the representative function. The role of the executive is not obvious, but it involves preparation of documents for the bidding and contract approval procedures. The executive makes arrangements as for necessary meetings, consultations, and information transmission to the relevant parties. Professional expertise is required for the technical specification development and to insure that documents are legally sound and that architectural services and technical assistance are coordinated to insure that the bidding process is properly executed. The representative function is discharged by board members who legitimize the contract and assure the community that all provisions are in the interest of the school district. Others may enter the process to use data to inform the local citizenry of potential bidders, the bidding process, and the proper award. For example, media representatives who follow the process and report it to the community may legitimize this step. Throughout step five, the executive is responsible for the proper execution of the process and the recommendation of a competent contractor to the board.

Sometimes architects have a tendency to take over executive functions during this phase. Extensive involvement and knowledge about building design can encourage architects to act on behalf of the executive in bidding and contracting. Representative lobbying for bidders may also assume leadership. They may dictate the nature of the process, and may call for procedural safeguards. Executives maintain control if they anticipate these tendencies and insist on retaining procedural authority.

STEP SIX: FACILITY CONSTRUCTION

The next step in the sequential planning and building process is to construct the building. Several considerations are taken into account during this step. First, the school building is intended to enhance the community image in two ways: through its contribution to the educational program and through its visual appeal. Second, the school building should possess some modification. All instructional spaces should be capable of being altered in size and shape at a reasonable cost. All utilities should be easily accessible to all parts of a school building. The mechanical and electrical elements should be installed so as not to impede the relocation of interior partitions. Ceilings should be designed so as to facilitate changes within a school building. The type of lighting fixtures employed should not restrict the placement of interior walls within the building to any major extent. Finally, the design of the building should facilitate the installation of electronic devices in all parts of the structure (Abramson, 1983, 1984, 1986, 1985; Day, 1986).

Sampton and Landes (1957) refer to modifiability in terms of certain principles: adaptability, flexibility, expansibility, and contractibility (p. 170). They suggest a number of features to examine. The placement of the building on the site can have a bearing, as can the traffic pattern and location of corridors, the central-utility-core concept (or the multipurpose section of the building), and anticipation of new instructional technologies. Destructible or movable partitions and suspended ceilings are features that may be important. Anticipated usage in the future is important to consider.

During construction projects, Kutkat (1983) found that the biggest "budget bust" of all is change orders. By change orders, Kutkat means changes made on the building after construction begins. He advocates complete documentation for each change that is proposed. This is important for the school district because ultimately the superintendent accounts for all financial transactions relating to the construction project (see Epperson, 1983).

An important task for the contractor is the adherence to a time schedule (Knirk, 1979).

During actual construction of the building, the executive concentrates on budget allocation, the construction schedule, and coordinating the work of architects, contractors, and construction engineers. Work during this step is controlled mainly by professionals—architects, engineers, and educators—who oversee technical aspects of construction and assure that educational specifications are incorporated into the building. The representative function is generally peripheral, confined to concerns about the structure and the building process. Some groups may complain about construction noise and disturbance or perhaps praise the efficient manner in which the construction process is progressing. The executive is responsible for insuring that the approved design for the structure is adhered to and that the structure is built according to the planned budget and schedule.

STEP SEVEN: OCCUPYING THE BUILDING

Once the constructed building is ready for occupancy, the seventh step in the process is to occupy the building. Earthman (1987) recommends that various user orientation and public information programs be prepared and conducted. He makes several suggestions (1986) about a number of occupancy activities that may be conducted. A staff orientation may take place that includes building tours, in-service sessions with other educators, mock fire drills, discussions centering on floor plans, and question-and-answer sessions with the architect. A building dedication, an open house for parents, student orientation, building tours for the community, media publicity, and printed materials also serve to let the community know about the new school (Jilk, 1987; Council of Educational Facility Planners, International, 1985; MacConnell, 1957).

During this step, the executive emphasizes engaging school personnel, students, and parents in committing their loyalty and support to the school program, and it is the executive's responsibility to lead school personnel, students, and parents in the public acknowledgment of the completed building and to solidify their commitment to the project and to ensure their support in the future maintenance of the site. Professionals are called in to administer the proper ceremonial and ritual activities. Professionals may also advise the executive on how best to incorporate the various groups in the community for school support. Representatives such as school board members participate in the opening acitivities, showing their support for the facility and its mission. Other political and professional dignitaries are also included in these activities. Educators may assist in initiating the development of intellectual and schooling norms. Their presence and their expressed sentiments provide support for the school district.

STEP EIGHT: POSTOCCUPANCY EVALUATION

The eighth step in the process of constructing schools is the postoccupancy evaluation. Earthman (1985a) presents four reasons why a postoccupancy evaluation should be conducted: (1) to modify or correct an existing building; (2) to provide guidelines for future facilities; (3) to evaluate the programming criteria and design effectiveness; and (4) to gather data on how people use and respond to the building. Most authorities recommend that the initial evaluation take place one year after occupancy and then at intervals during the next five years (Earthman, 1985a).

For the postoccupancy evaluation, several types of data-gathering instruments may be used, such as observational schedules and questionnaires. School-building survey specialists have made significant contributions to the present state-of-the-art of facilities evaluation. Check lists, rating scales, workbooks, score cards, evaluation forms, and appraisal guides have been developed. Since the product of the school planning effort is the facility, two approaches have been used to determine the quality of the product. The first approach is to assign a total score for a perfect school building with specific scores given to each item related to a particular aspect of the school design. Subscores are assigned to each item by the evaluator and added to obtain the total score for a school plant. The second approach is to begin with a perfect score on each item and assign penalty points for each shortcoming observed. The score for a particular facility is obtained by subtracting the penalty score from the assigned perfect score for each item.

The objective of the evaluation of the school site in particular is to determine if the site is centrally located and easily accessible to the present and future population; removed from undesirable industry, business, and traffic; and large enough to meet educational needs. As a standard, an elementary school site should encompass ten acres plus one acre for each 100 students. The middle school site should be twenty acres plus one acre for each 100 students. High school sites require thirty acres plus one acre for each 100 students. All sites should also be large enough for future on-site expansion.

The school site should also be well-landscaped. The topography should be varied enough to provide the desired appearance but without steep inclines. Campus soil should be stable and free of erosion.

The structural and mechanical features are examined to determine if the structure meets or exceeds all barrier-free requirements. The foundations are checked to see if they are strong and stable. The exterior and interior walls are examined to see if they are free of deterioration. Roofs are examined for their soundness. The entrances and exits are to be located to permit traffic flow. The building "envelope" should meet energy-use code requirements. Walls should permit flexibility for a variety of class sizes. The interior should be free of toxic materials. The electrical service should be underground. The electrical controls should be safely protected from environmental hazards and human interference.

The structure is also evaluated to see if it is "educationally adequate." Educational adequacy means that the learning areas should be compatible with the state instructional ends. The appraisal criteria should determine whether or not the site and building are well-equipped (see Akers, 1984; Hawkins, 1977; Hawkins and Lilley, 1986; Keck, 1978; McGuffey, 1974; Reida, 1962; Strayer and Engelhardt, 1923; Samption and Landes, 1957).

During the postoccupancy evaluation, the primary executive function is judgment, the professional function is inspection, and the representative function is accountability. Professionals, such as engineers, may be enlisted to examine specific aspects of the structure or to evaluate potential changes to identified problem areas. Educational personnel may be solicited for their professional judgment on issues such as the design of the library or science and technology laboratories. Representatives, such as parents and professional or civic associations (e.g., the PTA or Lions Club) may be invited to tour the plant to express their views on adequacy, usefulness, or innovativeness. Throughout this process the executive monitors the evaluations provided and ultimately approves the building or requests changes.

During this step, professionals may assume leadership when school facilities' specifications are found to be faulty. For example, a site's grading results in flooding and drainage problems. Engineers may assume dominance as they seek to satisfy angry parents or frustrated school personnel. Representatives may assume dominance as the media is called in to expose the problem.

STEP NINE: SCHOOL FACILITY USE

The ninth step in the process of constructing schools is building use. Minzey and Townsend (1984) and Hill (1983) express concern over the use of school buildings. Minzey and Townsend suggest that buildings be designed around a "core," which would be permanent and would house such community areas as the gymnasium, pool, library, meeting rooms, cafeteria, auditorium, and community office space. The remainder of the school (what Minzey, Townsend, and Hill refer to as the "plus") are those areas of the facility, such as classrooms, that are temporary in nature and can be increased or eliminated as the needs of the community change (p. 19). Hill (1984) in a similar manner writes that "educational facility planning can no longer be administered independently of surrounding social, economic, or political forces. Instead, it should be planned, programmed, and implemented jointly" (p. 4).

In order to deal with issues of shared use, the traditional practice has been to lodge the responsibility for the management of multiuse school buildings with district personnel. Ayres (1984) reported that the establishment of an interagency planning process is ideal. There are two major obstacles in multiple use of school buildings: (1) the "traditions" that exist in the use of school buildings, and (2) the funding of those buildings (Lutz et al., 1987, p. 3; Stewart, 1985; Swenson, 1987). Ayres found that the use of formal policy boards and working task forces to negotiate multiuse policy decisions lead to increased availability of educational facilities, enhanced revenue potential from building use, and improved facility design.

One study (Nisbet et al., 1980) is reported that attempted to use school buildings as community buildings. The study was conducted in Scotland. Two assumptions guided the research and the project. The first was to extend educational opportunities across age and class levels, and the second was to provide an institution that encouraged education as a lifelong process. The report indicates that integration of school facilities with community use is a complex process, primarily because bringing together two groups—teachers and community education workers—with different perspectives has the potential for conflict.

The Organization for Economic Cooperation and Development

(1978) undertook a Programme on Educational Building (PEB) between 1972 and 1981. The member countries—Australia, Austria, Belgium, Canada, Denmark, Finland, France, the Federal Republic of Germany, Greece, Iceland, Ireland, Italy, Japan, Luxemberg, the Netherlands, New Zealand, Norway, Portugal, Spain, Sweden, Switzerland, Turkey, the United Kingdom, the United States, and the Socialist Federal Republic of Yugoslavia—reported their country's construction practices and use of schools. The most significant conclusion they arrived at in the report is that "building use is related to the planning and design process and the development of relationships between those who planned and built the school and those who will use it" (p. 189). They refer to each facility as having its own magnetic field. That is, each facility is attached to its own community.

Finally, Kowalski (1989) explains that the expanding usage of schools is driven by two considerations: escalating taxes which encourage citizens to expect more benefits from the investment in school building, and increasing acceptance of lifelong learning and new values that make school and community inseparable (see Council of Educational Facility Planners, International, 1980).

During the building-use step, the executive is responsible for deciding whether and how to expand the building's use and when to share the building with others. The executive's function is to negotiate among competing interests and insure that educators' expertise is dominant in the considerations for these buildings. It is the executive who decides whether the building would be used for year-round or extended-day and -week use. It is also the executive who guides representative boards in deciding who should share the school building with the district. The executive determines how to cover or recover costs incurred from multiple-use of the school building—the executive may call on professionals such as recreational personnel for advice about extended use, or call on professionals for guidance about day care or other uses of the facility. Professional child development specialists and legal authorities may be counselled regarding liability and safety measures. Representative groups—the school board or parent groups—often influence the scope or regulations for multiple use of buildings. Representatives from local agencies create the demand for facility use. In the end, school building use acknowledges the representative function by advocating the use of public dollars to share public educational facilities.

Several generalizations may be drawn from the review of the literature. First, the steps required to construct new schools are well-identi-

FIGURE 5
Review of the Literature
Theoretical Framework

Steps	Executive	Professional	Representative	Literature
Needs Assessment	Initiative	Demographic Analysis	Recognition	Involvement Advocated
Long-range Plan	Organization	Advisory	Legitimacy/ Direction	Covered in Literature
Fiscal Plan	Decision Making	Technical Assistance	Mobilize Support	GOBs Calif. State Lit.
Building Design	Integration	Technical Assistance	Preference Representation	Steps Separate Functions and Conflict
Contract Bidding	Authorization	Expertise	Legitimation	Technical Literature
Construction Management	Supervision	Expertise	Legitimation Support	Technical Literature
Occupy	Leadership	Administration	Support	Technical Task
Evaluate Building	Judgement	Inspection	Accountability	Task Completion Without Judgment
Building Use	Negotiation	Advice	Advocacy	Small body of research. No mention of functions.

fied and -presented. The functions necessary to perform the steps are less well-understood. The executive function is recognized, but enactment of this role is left to individual interpretation. The call for professional expertise is also clear, but it is generally discussed in relationship to the technical nature of particular aspects of the steps rather than with the overall flow of the process. The role of democratic representation is acknowledged in the literature, but its contribution is perceived as general involvement, rather than as an integral component in the process. (See MacConnell, 1957, pp. 77-78).

The textbook literature does not address school-district/state relationships in the conduct of constructing new schools. The literature dealing with California school facility funding presents technical, legal, and fiscal information but neglects to distinguish between regulatory, fiscal, and distributive bases for associating. The present study intends to show, theoretically and practically, how the state and the school district relate to each other.

The interorganizational and interpersonal dimension associated with the relationship between the state and school district are not addressed in the literature. This study will show how differing motivations on the part of the state and the school district determine the interpersonal interaction that takes place between the state and school district officials. The consequence of this relationship is the school district's appointment of the person who fulfills the executive function.

Figure 5 summarizes the coverage of the theoretical framework in the literature.

Part II

Data Analysis

Chapter 3

Preconstruction Considerations

INTRODUCTION

As stated previously, school construction is a major project that school districts assume. The literature dealing with educational facilities refers to the term *project* as parts of the school facilities program. For example, Strevell and Burke (1959) define "project" as "(1) site acquisition, expansion, or improvement, (2) an improvement in, alteration of, addition to, or other change in an existing structure, or (3) a new structure to replace an existing facility or to add capacity to available facilities" (p. 4). They distinguish "project" from "program" by defining "program" as a "plan for meeting all of the needs for school facilities in a school system through one or more projects" (p. 4).

I am defining "project" as the totality of activities involved in the process of constructing new schools. The conceptualization of "project management" is that activity the school district assumes when it determines that schoolhousing needs to be provided. The process commences with the assessment of need and terminates with the determination of school-building use. The collapsing of all of these activities is useful because it provides parameters around the activity while linking all of its parts. As is evident from the definitions presented above, school construction is more likely to be seen in fragments if projects are specified within the program rather than as a total project consisting of steps (placing it more as a process). When the process of constructing new schools is embarked upon, the school district's activities and structure are affected.

THE FACILITIES PLANNER

School districts are organizationally structured to carry out day-to-day activities. When they embark upon educational facility construction, the usual first step is to appoint someone to direct the activity, usually a facilities planner. But many districts, especially smaller ones, redirect the responsibilities of facility planning to one of their in-house officials. The literature reports that facilities planners are apt to be individuals who worked their way up through the ranks of the school system (Kowalski, 1989, p. 142). When school facilities were to be built, facilities planners assumed the responsibility for the project. Today, facility management is normally viewed as requiring more than technical skills. The individual in charge is expected to understand policy development and interpretation, have the ability to supervise and evaluate employees, and possess skills for formulating and administering budgets (Kowalski, 1989, p. 142). In sum, what is called for in facilities planners is a manager of a project. In reference to the theoretical framework, this manager is the executive.

Out of the twenty school districts examined in this study, six had experienced facilities planners. Eleven districts had facilities planners new to their district, and three districts had others acting as facilities planners (two districts' superintendents and one district's retired associate superintendent of business).

School district facilities planners describe their roles with differing emphasis on a variety of responsibilities. The most comprehensive description of the role was presented by an acting facilities planner:

> My responsibilities would include any facilities planning. My role is to be constantly working with the architect and tracking new development and population trends and needs for new schools. In gaining site approval I accompany State Department of Education personnel on site visitations. After the specifications have been completed I work with the architect until all the technical work has been completed. I remain active in the bid award by reviewing with the architect the bids and making recommendations. Finally, I oversee the construction through the completion of the product.

Most facilities planners emphasize their involvement with new projects and demographic or enrollment projections. For example, one of the facilities planners described his role as "the primary person in charge of all new school projects. Demographic growth projections determine the needs from a district standpoint and I must determine those district areas subject to growth and new development."

Many of the facilities planners have other responsibilities besides facilities; for example, one facilities planner is also director of administrative services. He coordinates the project, works with the architect and the various local agencies, insures that building and maintenance are taken care of, and reports to the school board. Attending to other administrative services such as food and transportation are also part of his job.

Some facilities planners share their responsibilities with others. The facilities planner from Green Valley Unified School District explained that the previous superintendent had begun the process of building new schools because the district did not have a facilities planner until they were able to hire someone in September. After hiring the facilities planner she continued her involvement monitoring and meeting with him on a regular basis in joint and department meetings with the contractors, developers, architects, and the inspectors. She acts as the facilities planner's immediate supervisor as well as the authorized agent for the state school building projects and the community facilities district, signing all of the documents for the district and serving as the liaison between the projects and the board, and making all fiscal decisions and preparing all documents for board approval.

This sort of relationship to the facilities planner also exists in another school district, where the assistant superintendent for business assumes most of the facilities planner's responsibilities. The facilities planner in this school district helps the assistant superintendent for business by attending city planning meetings and other types of meetings that deal with developments within the district. He works with the developers until the situation is right for the assistant superintendent for business to meet with them and conclude a final settlement.

In Hidden Springs Unified School District the facilities planner serves as a coordinator, gets information from the commissions, and meets with internal committees. The deputy superintendent's office is responsible for the facilities meetings and for the spacework group-meetings.

The facilities planner from Cactus Ranch Unified School District had obtained her position a few months prior to the interview. She said,

> I was an executive secretary before, but because there was reliance on me to collect the information that facilities planners deal with, I could pick up the job. Actually, I had a lot of different functions. Before everyone did many things, but now we have more specialization and that is why I became facilities planner. This is a big job. Each facilities department functions differently. Some have maintenance. I do not; I have attendance. Most do not have that. We just do the best we can.

Because a good portion of the facilities planners in this sample were new to the position, many of them referred to their previous experiences in explaining how they understand their work. The University City facilities planner was an administrative assistant in a facility planning unit several years before becoming secretary to the superintendent. From this position she was appointed facilities planner after most of the planning for one of the elementary schools had been done. She summarized, "Of all the things that a planner needs, I wish that I had teaching experience. I wish I knew more about what teachers need. There are a lot of us who have different backgrounds. Some of us are in business, planning, construction, and education. The job entails all of the above."

The description presented above indicates that school construction is not normally conceived as a project requiring a special task force. Instead, the process is viewed as a collection of activities and responsibilities to be assumed by someone within the school district on a temporary basis. Even though the facilities planner role is that of an executive, coordinating the critical actors, tasks, and operations to assure that facilities are built on schedule in a cost-efficient manner, its temporariness is maintained when placed in more than one person. The newness of the job, the inexperience of the planner, and the extent to which others in the district relate to the facilities planner determine the degree to which the executive function can be fulfilled. The executive function is, thus, complicated to the degree that the role is enacted by more than one actor. The faithfulness with which the process of constructing schools is carried out is largely determined by the form in which the executive function is fulfilled. The next section presents the steps that are necessary to build new schools and how the executive function interacts with the professional and representative functions.

SCHOOL CONSTRUCTION PROCESSES

As has been presented above, the need for school facilities is great in the nation. School districts can respond to this need in a number of ways. They may ignore the need and cope with inadequate buildings and overcrowded classrooms, or readjust school schedules to enable students to attend through year-round or double-session schedules. They may choose to add relocatables to their sites until their space is exhausted. For elementary schools they may also order standardized, prefabricated, factory-built schools. Districts tend to consider all of the above solutions as temporary. The permanent solution is to construct new facilities.

School districts construct school facilities through a process consisting of nine steps, which take place sequentially, with a beginning and ending point, but sometimes overlap. Each step proceeds to the next step because the responsibilities and the composition of the three functions differ. The first step is needs assessment.

NEEDS ASSESSMENT

The need for school facilities arises from three basic sources: the replacement of existing buildings, the movement of groups from one area to another (such as the influx of immigrants or families seeking relocation), and new development. Currently, the three sources of need are critical.

Each source of need requires a different mode for assessing the need and acquiring official school board approval for the construction of new facilities. The most common need and the one that is most demanding on the district and state is the need arising from new development. How that need is assessed will be presented first.

New development creating need

The needs assessment process includes fundamental information: tract maps of development; development type to determine housing and student ratio; district's capacity to absorb, expand, or build additional facilities; California Basic Educational Data (CBEDS) information; cohort survival computation, and determination of classroom space needed.

The needs assessment process involves a number of critical steps. The district initiates the process through the facilities planner. The facilities planner determines the need by looking at some indicators. One of the first indicators to arrive at his or her desk is the tract map from the county office. This document details projected development and requests for permission to build.

The tract map shows the development that is taking place but may not provide all of the necessary information for the facilities planner to make informed decisions. The type of projected development and type of housing will give some indication about the number and age of children. That information is, then, used to determine if schools need to be expanded or built, and what levels need to be addressed.

One of the questions school districts confront is whether they will have adequate time to construct their school so that the building will be ready when the children move in to the development. Linking the projected development, the approval date for the development, and the developers' timetable to the district's involvement assists the district in coordinating its building with that of the developers. This is problematic because the facilities planner and the office responsible for granting permission for the development do not always share information. The information is important for the facilities planner because the need is validated, the location of greatest impact is identified, and the developer might help in funding the school.

The process by which need is determined varies because granting permission for development does not always result in development. Also, many times the projected time period for developing is underestimated or overestimated. Some facilities planners resort to their own means of tracking potential developments. For example, the facilities planner from Cozy Corner Unified School District described his process as follows:

> We keep very close contact with all builders to determine growth. We call two or three times a year to check what has been going on. We are particularly interested in the summertime because two out of three times our growth will take place during that time. That is when people move into their new homes. The county requires we be notified whenever a new development begins. Maps need to be approved once they are here. Once they start grading we contact them. From then on, we try to stay on top of the development. We ask, "How many homes will be opening when?"

In brief, when new development has been assured, the school district is then able to begin its process of validating its need for new school construction. The formal means for attaching development to new school need is through legislation that allows the district to connect itself to the new development process. The developers are subsequently required to contact the district in order to know which school the children within that development project will attend. They are also required to be able to inform parents accurately about the school placement of their children. The facilities planner from Cactus Ranch Unified School District explained how they work with the developer in order to establish need:

> The Project Rancho is a development in which 15,540 homes are to be built. They contacted the district three years ago when they began. The facilities planner looked at the housing patterns and where the developers were asking for permits. The facilities planner determined where the activity is taking place. The city is, then, contacted to find out what is happening. A large project calls for a group to meet and discuss how a school is required. The facilities planner tries to influence developers to decide a school project is required and the developer agrees to the fees. The city about two weeks ahead of time will

send this agenda to the facilities planner. A response is sent and the committee members are informed prior to the meeting. After several times of working with developers, by now some projects are more positive towards the construction of schools than others and we have a more stable system of informing each other.

Once it is determined that a new school is needed, the district then calculates its classroom space requirement. The facilities planner from Green Valley District described how classroom space determination takes place.

> The district's interest is in how many houses, the size and cost of the houses. Right now the district is yielding about 1.8 children per home. This is running about .90-.95 K-6; the balance is broken up in mid-high and high. As an example, 1000 tract homes would produce about 950 children. The district policy is to house 720 children so that means the tract will demand a 3600-3700 square foot school K-6. Relocatables are needed to house an additional 180 children. Thirty children can be placed in a relocatable. That means 6 relocatables are needed. The total is 720 capacity K-6 school with 6 relocatables.

If the developer participates from the beginning, the district is more apt to receive site, financial, and completion date cooperation. One reason some of the sites have not utilized the process in this manner is because, as one facilities planner said, "The information coming from the county office is the slowest type of notification to reach the district. Big developers typically hire planning companies who contact the school district early on in the planning."

Another reason the process does not move as expeditiously and smoothly as it could is because counties and cities have different means of communicating to the district in regard to the development taking place. The facilities planner from Distant Place Unified School District described what happens in his district:

> Counting building structures in new housing areas and consulting with the local planning commission are the various methods we use. Since the school district collects its own builder's fees, the developers deal with the district directly in order to meet the county building requirement. The determination of geographical growth is made by graphing the data according to square miles. They follow a generation factor for K-6 grades which is 1/3 student per dwelling unit.

Hidden Springs Unified School District, on the other hand, has the facilities planner in direct contact with the county. The Associate Superintendent for Budgeting explained,

I have reporting to me a facilities planner who coordinates with city and county planners so that we get all the tract maps, and we know where all the development is going on. They put all of their work together in a system to allow them to determine the new tracts and number of units and where all the yield of students will come from.

Cozy Corner Unified School, on the other hand, recruits its transportation personnel to alert the facilities planners about the progress in development. They keep a historical account of the development and completion dates in order to more accurately assess how much time they have for their own building completion. The facilities planner explained how they calculate cohort survival rates: "We take all of our kindergartners and make them first graders; we drop out the twelfth grade; we project kindergartners and then we apply what we think is a legitimate growth factor to that." Finally, they use CBEDS information to verify.

Small school districts apply a personalized process. Retreat Unified School District's facilities planner explained,

> Our district personnel drive around and tally new housing starts. The developers come to the district office to pay their fees. Currently, the development is taking place in the northern part of the district. This growth, however, is small 2-5 house starts, spotty and leaving much acreage still open. South of a major highway three large developments are opening up in the next year. They each comprise approximately 1200-1500 acres with 2300-4500 buildings. One of the developments is located along the highway and will include a lot of commercial businesses, whereas another will have all single family dwellings.

Some school districts see the gradual growth of their community and begin to plan for new schools a decade in advance. They determine whether they need land or sites for additional schools and they try to project a means for gathering support and funds. University Unified School District's superintendent determined before developer fees existed and before the onslaught of development that the eastern corner of the city would develop and require facilities. The facilities planner explained how this process took place.

> The superintendent began negotiations in 1982 with East Ranch to get the property. The agreement with East ranch was settled and dated February 1987. He and the Assistant Superintendent met with people from East Ranch before we had developer fees and the agreement we formulated gave us the site.

University City's experience illustrates the importance of the linkage between new development and the provision of new schoolhousing. Being out in front too far in advance of the projected development, however, resulted in miscalculating the location of the schools. The facilities planner said,

> The school district decided that this location was not the best location for a new school. East Ranch, a local corporation, is developing the whole area and the school district traded the ten-acre site down the street for this ten-acre site plus several hundred thousand dollars. It also kept a fifteen-year lease on the elementary school located there. When the new school opens, they will still have eleven years left on their lease. The district has not decided how it will use the lease. Originally, the plan was to build a new school for six hundred kids.

A different sort of problem arises when the growth spans more than one district. The two districts have to agree that one or the other will build the school to absorb the children from the adjoining district. Likewise, the community spanning both districts has to agree to support the agreement. The developer, likewise, concurs with the community and districts regarding the location and ownership of the school. In this case the need for facilities and eventual location become important considerations for both the school districts and developer.

When new development creates the need for new schools, the demographic data are available in the county, city, and developers' offices. Ideally, the process for the construction of schools and the rest of the development would be occurring simultaneously. However, as our data indicate, the independence of all parties has complicated the process, and schoolhousing needs are not always being met.

As was presented at the beginning of this section, certain types of information, action, and actors are necessary when the need for new schools is created by new development. The facilities planner must be able to obtain and comprehend tract maps of development and be able to generate the appropriate student-ratio formulas that correspond to the type of housing being constructed in the new development. The facilities planner needs to have available a current profile regarding the school district's capacity to house the projected enrollment; must acquire, comprehend, and integrate the CBEDS information with their own district's capacity; compute the cohort survival rate; and, finally, determine the classroom space needed. The facilities planner can engage demographers; school personnel; state, city, and county officials; and others in order to prepare a statement of need regarding school facilities created by new development.

Displacement creating need

The school construction process differs when the need for new schools is created by shifts of differing socioeconomic groups to older parts of the city. Growth resulting from population shifts takes place when multiple families move into single-family dwellings. This practice contributes to an underestimation of their presence. This group, moreover, is not as demanding as the new development one. Relocatables are the primary means by which schoolhousing is provided for this group. One of the officials from Hidden Springs Unified School District voiced this problem:

> The minorities that make up that figure do not want to vote. They do not follow the schools. They produce kids. The city is getting the multifamily-per-dwelling-unit problem in the older homes. The growth is at the rate of about two schools a year and it takes three and a half years to build a school. Just to do the paperwork. It is a no-win situation. Portables are being placed on all the schools. The district has 129 portables now and is looking for 40 more to go up next week. These units are becoming permanent. The district has portables which have been in place for eleven years. Once they are brought on, it seems to be impossible to replace or be rid of them.

In order for facilities planners to justify new school buildings in these areas, they need to have information regarding the shift of population and its magnitude. County, city, and other social services agencies obtain information regarding these shifts but are not obligated to report it to school districts. School districts become aware of these shifts when children show up at the neighborhood school's door. A systematic count of this population shift would facilitate the determination of schoolhousing need.

Facilities built to replace others were not identified in the data collected. However, relocatables have been brought to virtually all sites in all districts to enable expansion, and one-third of all new facility building must be relocatables. Thus, flexibility in each site is being built in to adjust to further growth or decline as necessary. More about this is presented in the section dealing with the fiscal planning stage.

Recognition of need

Once the facilities planner has gathered all of the necessary information from the various agencies and has devised or designed a projection of facilities need, he or she seeks acknowledgment of the need by the school board and community.

In most cases, a committee consisting of school personnel and community individuals participate in some manner. Minimally, they are informed about the need for facilities and how it was determined. The school board is always the body that recognizes the need in a formal way. Usually, the recommendation by the facilities planner to fulfill the need is accepted by the board and community.

In our study, University City did not accept the recommendation from the facilities planner and the board president. The board president explained,

> One of our problems is that the community does not want a separate high school. They would just as soon have six thousand kids at only one high school, because then there is only one football team. It is a real difficult problem for community citizens to realize that it is okay to have two high schools.

As the need for new schools, funding, and accuracy of projections has increased, the county offices have become more active in providing support and help to school districts. One of the county officers explained, "I see my job as one of advisor as well as one who certifies district average daily attendance (ADA). I use the OLA software program to determine cohort survival, calculate future enrollment, and help facilitate the district's progress. As we meet with others in the district we learn and support each other." This type of cooperation between the school district and agencies ensures that the need for new school buildings is acknowledged.

Conclusions

The establishment of need requires specialized information and linkages in order to assure the provision of school facilities in a timely fashion and in the proper locations. That specialized information is not readily available to school districts. The executive, in this case the facilities planner, must rely on "bits of information" from multiple sources, which are then compiled and analyzed and acted upon by the district. Because the bits of information "trickle in" and because the facilities planner is not a demographer, the information is acted upon practically rather than comprehensively.

The school board and community have the same information the facilities planner does and their participation may or may not be supportive. For example, the wide disparity in community involvement may be an indication that both the facilities planner and the community have equal access to essentially the same information upon which the decision for the construction of schools is based. Facilities planners do not present their request for new facilities based on a specialized body of information that justifies new facilities. Agreement for new facilities is granted when it is obvious a new development is large enough for a facility. The community perceives the existing facilities as adequate, and until new development and enrollment increases convince it otherwise, support for new facilities for new development is problematic.

The data for this report indicate that in order to conduct this step in the process of constructing new schools, specialized information and the need for a demographer who can not only determine growth but can compile the necessary information to specify the type, the speed, and its volatility are necessary.

This step also requires that development be linked to the provision of schoolhousing. At the present time, developers are required to conduct an environmental impact assessment. Part of that assessment can be the provision of schoolhousing. Several outcomes can be determined. First, neighborhood ownership of the school takes place. Second, the financing of the building is assumed by the affected group. Third, the interdependence of the relevant parties gets established in a systematic and enduring manner.

Finally, information regarding population shifts needs to be transmitted to those agencies who are responsible for integrating those families within the city. Multiple families in single dwellings must be accounted for in a more systematic way and the response to their needs must be immediate in order to ensure their political and social involvement. As these steps are being taken, the school district is integrated into the process to ensure that the children are provided with adequate schoolhousing.

The replacement of existing facilities is not part of this report.

LONG-RANGE PLANNING

After the need for additional schoolhousing has been acknowledged, the district proceeds to the second step, the preparation of the long-range plan. Most school districts have five-year plans, referred to as master plans, which may or may not include facilities planning. Because the state agencies, OLA and CSDE/SFPD, were requiring long-range plans when the study first started, all of the facilities planners who were interviewed had a plan that corresponded to the required form. Some school districts had their own long-range plans and a few had long-range facilities plans.

The facilities planner from Cozy Corner Unified School District described their process:

> Our five-year master plan, longer than that sometimes, is based on our projections. We decide what schools are needed and when. For example, in our district the next three schools will be two elementary schools and a middle school based on the new development and the capacity for our district to absorb the growth. The district pulls in members from the community to work with the architect and the staff to determine what kinds of school the district should have. Currently, our projections for the next five years is $78 million. Of that we project we can raise $13 million from the local developers and $65 from the voters' authorization.

School districts adhered to the requirement for state funding by projecting facility needs and justifying their inability to absorb the projected growth in a formal report that was cumbersome to compile and of questionable usefulness. It was eventually dropped from the process as a recommendation from the Price-Waterhouse Report.

Our data in this study indicate that the utility of the long-range plan is in justifying the linkage between the development and shifting population processes to the school construction process. When school districts can clearly demonstrate their inability to absorb the growth resulting from new development or shifting population, developers and others are more likely to support school construction. The facilities planner's role at this stage is greatly diminished without the long-range plan document. His or her ability to organize and mobilize the district and others is compromised to the degree that she or he cannot provide information as required. Without a long-range plan the school board and community are unable to furnish legitimacy.

The facilities planner enacts the executive function by organizing the information that is necessary and presenting the information to the school board and community. The professionals provide advice while the representatives provide legitimacy and direction. The close of this step is signified when the board approves the long-range plan and directs the facilities planner to proceed with the fiscal plan.

FISCAL PLANNING

The magnitude of cost is the main reason that facility planning is one of the most critical activities in which school districts engage. When the need for school facilities escalates in the manner it has during the past decade, calls for relief come from many sources. Boyer (1983, p. 295) wrote

The federal government has a leading role to play in rebuilding the nation's schools. A new federal program, The School Building and Equipment Fund, should be established to provide short-term, low-interest loans to schools for plant rehabilitation.

California's facilities needs

The elevation of school buildings to an importance for which the citizenry must assume responsibility and commitment is necessary. Although the entire nation is currently experiencing the need for school facilities, it is greater in the state of California; for not only is there a need to replace facilities, there is also a need to provide new facilities due to new development and population displacement. The data (California Basic Educational Data System, or CBEDS) show that the total number of public schools increased from 7,237 in 1988-89 to 7,358 in 1989-90, and comparable yearly growth is expected through the mid nineties.

The enrollment figures reported in 1991 show 4,618,120 in 1988-89; 4,771,978 in 1989-90, and 4,950,474 in 1990-91. It is projected that 5,139,000 students will enroll in 1991-92, and by 1995-96, 5,977,000 students will be enrolled (Heydt, 1991, p. 4).

California's school facilities funding plans

As is common in most states, funding for schools comes from a variety of sources. Aside from the state funding program (the LeRoy Greene Lease-Purchase Program), California has sought many types of funding plans. Even though the examples presented here come from the state of California, the sources of funding are common across the nation. States tend to support a portion of funding. General Obligation Bonds (GOBs) are the most common source of funding and there are a variety of other financial packages that are available in most states. The analysis presented is designed to provide general and theoretical understanding. The California state data (Heydt, 1991, p. 1) indicate that between 1983 and 1990, 124 elections were called for GOBs, representing 12.3 percent of the state's districts. Half of them were successful. The second most common plan adopted by school districts, the Mello-Roos plan, indicate that thirty-six Mello-Roos funding proposals were attempted and ten passed.

There are several ways of collecting moneys for new schools. First, there are developer fees. If a house is being built, a set of plans is submitted to the county. There is a tax per square foot (developer fees) that must be paid to the schools before the plans can be out of plan check. For example, if a contractor comes in to build one hundred houses, the money associated with the square footage of all the houses is paid up front.

A second way is through Mello-Roos, in which the builder places some money up front and the money is then taxed on those people who are going to live in those houses. A third way is through GOBs, obtained by elections. Finally, the district can look at the process of land banking. That means going through a corporation and attempting to purchase all of the school district's projected sites at today's prices rather than trying to buy them in the future at whatever those prices will be. It will not cost the district any money up front. The state will then buy back those lots under the state funding program at whatever the going rate is. So, the district stands to gain a few extra dollars for constructing more schools.

After the passage of Proposition 13, school districts directed their requests for school facilities funding to the state. Because the period of dramatic growth was preceded by a period of stability and decline, most school districts did not have the personnel and resources to handle the demands placed upon them. Even though OLA, the state regulatory agency responsible for facilitating the process for the acquisition of funds, assumes the responsibility for educating, preparing, and previewing the necessary steps for successful completion of the process, many districts lacked the awareness necessary for expedient processing of the funding. An official from OLA gives classes to architects and school personnel. Additionally, SAB, the agency that disburses the funds, holds a board meeting every month to update the process. After each board meeting, the OLA official meets with district representatives to discuss policy changes and other items. There are over 1200 districts and about 1 percent of them keep up with the policy changes normally explained during these meetings.

State agencies act as overseers to the construction of facilities process. OLA looks at cost effectiveness and OLA and OSA evaluate every set of plans as if it were new because, even though school districts are encouraged to submit standard rather than original designs, structural and safety changes are continually taking place. Architects become involved and design schools to meet the specifications and standards required by the various state agencies that guide school construction.

The state funding program, the LeRoy Greene Lease-Purchase Program, requires a process organized into phases. Moneys are allocated with each phase as it is approved. Phase 1 covers request and approval of application for funds. Phase 2 covers the approval of the fiscal plan, site, design, educational specification, and bid. Phase 3 covers the contract award, approval, and postoccupancy evaluation of the building. OSA can delay approval of Phase 2 when there is no money available. If the district has not been able to use the money allocated in Phases 2 or 3, or has been delayed by OSA, or for some other reason the process has not been continued, then SAB may reclaim the money.

When a district requests funding and there isn't any, it gets placed on an official information list acting to provide SAB reimbursement. Funds that have been approved by SAB are guaranteed. However, the current lack of funds has halted further funding. The School Finance Committee can authorize selling from the Bond Act when the funds are available to the Department of the Treasury. SAB keeps $15 million on reserve for modernization projects. An alternative is for school districts to accept relocatables.

Because the state does not have enough money and because the need for new schools is associated with new development, school districts are required to collect developer fees to match state-allocated moneys. If SAB funds Phase 1, the application triggers the developer-fees matching-plan and locks the district into it regardless of future funding. The match is limited to the apportionment and the phase. In other words, if the apportionment is for Phase 1 moneys, then the match is for no more than that. This also enables the district to proceed with other moneys from other sources. Subsequently, these moneys, when used, will then be reimbursed when and if SAB regains its funds. SAB encourages districts to use these options, but there is a perception among some districts that SAB funds school construction without the enforcement of the use of optional sources. Conversely, the state agencies perceive that often districts use these alternative funding methods to pay other debts.

In 1982, Mello-Roos was established to aid with local funds and tie the funding to the source of need. The districts assume full responsibility for acquiring these funds because the county treasurers did not want the responsibility.

In 1986, Proposition 14 reestablished districts' ability to have GOBs that are processed through the county. The joint agreements, such as redevelopment, with the city are handled through the city's treasury, where these bonds are deposited and invested.

School districts have banded together in organizations such as the Coalition for Adequate School Housing (CASH), The California Association of School Budget Officers (CASBO), and the Schools Legal

Defense Association (SLDA). They are designed to provide districts the means to communicate with each other and with the legislature regarding funding for new schools.

The facilities planner from Cactus Ranch explained their district's participation:

> We belong to CASH. I attend a lot of their meetings and I attend their conferences because they tend to focus on different things. I just go to those which I think will help me in my work. The topic is what alerts you to their usefulness. The best thing about these groups is that they inform you. So much happens so fast that it is difficult to stay on top of all of the information. People come to share information.

School district fiscal planning analysis

The previous section has dealt with general funding issues as faced by school districts across the state of California. Other states have similar issues and similar sources of funds. In order to understand the seriousness and facets of the process of funding new facilities, data from the sampled school districts will be presented in this section. School districts' facilities planners are the persons directly involved with the process. They enact the executive function, relying heavily on legal and financial experts or professionals. The importance of the representative function in providing support by appearing and disappearing throughout the process is demonstrated.

The cases presented illustrate the composition of actors in the various funding programs school districts put together and the means by which they are coordinated.

Dr. Denton, the facilities planner of Dry Lake Union High School District described the funding situation that not only represents his district but most of the California Educational Research Cooperative (CERC) membership districts. Prior to Proposition 13, a two-thirds passage of a GOB was required from the voters, and if the bond did not provide sufficient funds, a combination of local GOBs and state money became the standard way school districts financed their new schools. In Dr. Denton's words,

> Proposition 13 was such a watershed event. Since 1978 we have been in "some state of chaos." My opinion is that one effect of Proposition 13 was to take away the ability to go for local GOBs. By state consitutional amendment about three years ago, local GOBs have been restored. Two-thirds vote is still needed but difficult to obtain. The state has had to "bail out" the school districts for operating expenses.

Two school districts represent successful state funding. Green Valley Unified School District built two elementary schools with state funding prior to the full housing development. Its subsequent requests for additional schools have been delayed until funds are available.

The facilities planner from the Hanging Bridge Unified School District explained that there are similarities and differences in the growth patterns of two decades ago and now. Before Proposition 13, the school district and community were able to fund the new school buildings. In contrast, today the district does not have enough assessed value to pass a GOB, so all new building is entirely dependent on the state funding process. Fortunately, the Hanging Bridge School District requested state funding at the right time. Three of the district's proposed schools were fully funded this year and only one school remains to be funded. Hanging Bridge High School was eight weeks behind in the process to receive funding, forcing it to be placed on the information list and delaying its opening by one year or until the state resumes funding.

Obtaining General Obligation Bonds (GOBs). Fiscal planning at the school districts includes a process for obtaining funds. As explained with the two examples presented above, the usual method after Proposition 13 was to go to the state. But the state expended all of its funds while most of the school districts in the area were just beginning to assess the need. Other sources have had to be identified and pursued. Cozy Corner Unified School District provides an example where GOBs became their major source of funding for their extensive building program.

Fiscal planning for Cozy Corner Unified School District is a complicated process. The facilities planner elaborated:

> Currently, we do not have state funding for the next three schools. The state is out of money and does not plan on having any money available until June 1990. That puts us into a situation of having to search for alternative means for funding our schools. On June 30th, our school board called for an election, November 7th, to ask for a general obligation bond. We are going that route now. We are asking for $65 million. If we are successful in November, we will be able to sell bonds by March 1990. Also, if we are successful in November, we will go ahead and start our bidding process, and be ready to award a bid when the money is there. If we can award a bid in March, we will have the facilities ready to open in the fall of 1991. The GOB process is much simpler. You still have to deal with the State, the OSA, and the CSDE/SFPD. The educational needs are still to go through the CSDE,

no matter who funds the school facilities. The state has to know you are complying with the safety regulations and structural requirements. But you are not dealing through that financial uncertainty and paperwork to get state funding.

Besides the facilities planner, other school administrators were engaged in the pursuit of funds for new schools. The principal from Daisy Middle School and the superintendent were involved in pursuing funds resulting in success. The superintendent quoted from the local newspaper:

> The first school bond to be passed in the county since 1977 approved a $38.5 million GOB with 71.4 percent of the vote to construct a high school. In the city of Cozy Corner, 70.2 percent of the voters supported a $65 million measure to build a handful of schools including a second high school.

The GOB financing is handled at the county level. When bonds are sold, authorization to go ahead and sell the bonds over a five-year period is granted. Those proceeds are deposited in the county treasurer's office. Then they are disbursed in a manner similar to any other disbursement. The county serves as the fiscal agent but the district office is accountable for the funds.

Typically, school districts call for technical help from the state agencies, OLA and CSDE/SFPD. The architect deals directly with OSA and the Fire Marshall. Because most of the facilities planners are inexperienced with GOBs, school districts proceed with caution. The process by which the Cozy Corner Unified School District organized itself after passage of the GOB is described in apprehension by the facilities planner:

> The OSA is one of the big hangups in the whole process because they must approve all of the plans. Typically, things sit there for a long, long time. The Fire Marshall, CSDE/SFPD, and OSA are involved regardless of funding. Also, we do not know if OLA will try to be involved with GOB funding. The county treasurer's office, and the county superintendent's office are involved in the process. All of the books are maintained at the county superintendent's office. They do not give much advice though. The budget for building schools includes the cost of the land, architect, and everything.

In sum, this case shows how a GOB was successfully obtained, how it was integrated within the state guidelines, and how the various parties participated in a meaningful way. There was the active involvement of many school personnel besides the facilities planner. The board members played a "behind-the-scenes" role, whereas the administrators openly organized and made decisions regarding the facilities funding process. The facilities planner, although inexperienced, led the group. The technical actors were called in the order they were needed in the process.

Developer fees and state funding match. The case above illustrates successful passage of a GOB, but for some districts this is not a simple matter. The University Unified School District has been unable to pass a GOB after several attempts. The principal from one of the elementary schools explained how the funding process affected the building of his school.

> University has gone to the people twice in the last couple of years to try to get a bond issue to pay for three elementary schools and a high school. Unfortunately, the taxpayers did not see it that way. The bond almost passed, receiving 60% of the vote the first time and 64% the second time, which is almost two-thirds of the vote. After failing the two bond issues, we went to the state and asked, "If we raise half of the money we need, and only request half of the funds we need for our construction, will you move us up in the priority list?"
>
> The request was granted. The state allocated $22 million instead of $44. The funding for Green Wash Elementary is half from the state, $1 million from the East developer, and the remainder from the school district.

In comparing how Cozy Corner Unified School District and University Unified School District obtained funds, several important differences emerge. First, recall that University City's School officials had bought property early on and the location of that property was later found to be inadequate, whereas Cozy Corner acquired property after new development. Second, Cozy Corner is a developing community, representing new growth across the district. In contrast, University City has a historically well-established, stable section, and the need for a new school is primarily lodged on new development in a separate part of the city. Third, the school personnel led all of the GOB campaign activity throughout the Cozy Corner School District. The community participated, but the district was in command throughout. University Unified School District, on the other hand, played a less direct role. Parents played major roles, and in the second campaign district personnel retreated openly from the process. Fourth, the need for new school facilities existed across the Cozy Corner Unified School District, whereas the need in University City was localized. The total district was unable to assume the responsibility for the new growth. The limited executive leadership and school personnel participation reinforced the perception that new schools' need and source of funding be directly linked.

GOB funding requires participation from many sectors of the community and school organization. University Unified School District had an active parents group. Pamela, a parent from the University Unified School District described her involvement in the bond campaigns:

> We had a campaign committee consisting of school district personnel such as the top-level and area coordinators. I was involved with several aspects of fundraising. Each area was supposed to do a fundraiser and our area, East, held a very successful wine-tasting function. I acted as an area captain with volunteers who did the phone calling. As PTA president, I held meetings to explain the bond issue. This was very helpful because we were able to use our newsletter in relaying lots of information which rallied a lot of support. We were really proud because we passed the bond in our precinct, drawing an 89 percent yes vote.
>
> For the second bond election, the school district did not want any part of it, but did not discourage others. A group of about five or seven parents that were not school district employees got together and ran a very low cost campaign and actually did a little bit better than with the first one.

University Unified School District had not built a school in over two decades. Hardly anyone in the district had any experience with the process. University City also did not view providing schools for a new group of citizens as critical. Thus, the process for passing a GOB turned out to be impossible. Pamela explained,

> The city did not pass either bond because I do not think that even if the school district had been involved in the second campaign, it would have done any better. When I look back now, it was probably pretty futile to run the second bond campaign because they were so close together. The first one was in April and the second was in November. We did increase our vote but I think that there were still enough who were opposed. So, I do not think we would have benefitted much if the district had been more active. They did assist us; they held a poorly attended public forum. In a sense, we did have new areas pitted against old areas. The old areas in University City that are not experiencing growth and are stabilized do not see a need for new schools.

Another aspect illustrated in this case is how the community's involvement affects passage of GOBs. The two groups in University

City and the historical and social context of the city had a bearing on how the GOB process was affected. Pamela's historical analysis is that

> East was always very separate and distinct from Drake, and East associated with University, identified with it, and its children went to University schools, whereas Drake was completely separate. But University gave up this area and even though the majority of people up here wanted to incorporate into University, East has turned out to be a city consisting of very diverse areas with a history of conflict.

As presented in the theoretical framework, the representative function is to mobilize support for the acquisition of funds. In this case, the school board was unable to acquire this support—first, because the request was not viewed as legitimate; the need for new facilities was not being created by the general community, but by the newcomers. Second, the inability and, later, the retreat of the executive function from this process served to reinforce the separation between the established and new communities. Third, the need and source of funding were not immediately directly linked. The district, nevertheless, had to turn to the developers. University Unified School District was eventually successful in obtaining a portion of the needed funds from the developer for an elementary school, and the state agreed to match the developer's contribution. Developer fees seldom provide sufficient funds for a building. In this case, the facilities planner sought to swap and acquire land in order to successfully continue the process of building. The facilities planner explained,

> We are trying to sell a very small piece of land which adjoins somebody's personal property. We also have some land we are trying to swap. The state will allow you to exchange property more readily than to sell it and buy. We have a vacant elementary site in University which is next to a junior high that we are trying to trade for a site where we will have more room. We also have a high school site in Beautiful Hill which was not in a flood plane twenty years ago when it was purchased, but is now. Districts try to do this because they do not have to go to bidders or to the public. You just swap.

The case presented above shows a variety of ways in which parties within the district participate. The executive, professional, and representative functions are interdependent, and it is critical they remain distinct and active. When the executive relinquishes decision-making to the community, as in the GOB process, and when the executive tries to assume professional specialization, as with the developer fees, the process is disrupted.

Some districts have had more extensive experience with developer fees and have evolved a procedure that integrates developers into their new facilities planning program. The facilities planner from Cactus Ranch Unified School District described their funding process:

> We are involved in the Classroom Structure Authority (CSA) group. The city or county collect the developer fees. The CSA group does all of the accounting for us. We use the fees to buy or lease relocatable classrooms. In this way interim housing is being provided for the students. The growth is being handled in that way. Only the high-desert area or districts are in the CSA because our district is the largest district in this area. Starting from scratch we developed a plan. The difficulty has been that without big developers the growth has been sporadic and difficult to track.

Cactus Ranch Unified School District demonstrates how alternate funding increases the complexity of school construction. The facilities planner explained how the regulations the state imposes with state funding must be considered in alternate funding processes:

> For alternate funding the district need not contact OLA. The district must comply to state safety requirements. OSA is the agency involved. If alternate funding is used, OLA is not concerned with the class size nor square footage of facility. However, if at some later date this same district plans to use OLA funding, OLA will calculate eligible square footage by pooling all existing schools' square footage. This may work against the district, if they have built excessively using square footage calculations based on other than OLA standards.

Cactus Ranch Unified School District's success with developer fees may be lodged in many years of experience and in agreeing to interim relocatable housing while the state provides permanent housing. This district provides a good example of successful utilization of developer fees and state funding in its school construction program.

Independent district funding. Hidden Springs Unified School District is a district that has not availed itself of state funding. It has organized itself into various committees and groups, which search for funds from the various sources. For example, the person who acts as the facilities planner from the Hidden Springs Unified School District explained that there is a team of players that helps with the Mello-Roos financing:

> There is a legal board council consisting of a local law firm, a financial analyst, an assessment engineer, an underwriter, and a fiscal agent, a bank. When the bonds are sold they get deposited there and then the district draws against those bonds. Of course there is a paying agent

and a transfer agent on the board. Attorneys supervise all of that because no one at the state level is responsible. The state is aligned for the LeRoy Greene process, but if you acquire your own funds, you are on your own. The architect has to see that even though the school is built with Mello-Roos funds, it still, by law, has to comply to the LeRoy Greene state standards.

In this school district, the facilities planner, as assistant superintendent for business, is responsible for all finances. The entire accounting system is under him. Through an accountant, he also does the investments on outside tracts. The assistant superintendent for business takes care of all of this authorization, including buying necessary land. Each transaction must be approved by the board. The assistant superintendent for business is the designated agent for the board in two areas: as financial agent and as agent for negotiations with the developers for fees or donated land or whatever conditions need to be specified.

The sophisticated system of committee work, technological data processing, and district social network enabled this school district to build an elementary school with developer fees and district moneys. But in spite of its assets, the district housed one complete site with relocatables, engaged in a lengthy litigation with developers over another school site, and has been unsuccessful in forming a Mello-Roos community facilities district. What is demonstrated in this case is that interdependence based on funding creates problems and stresses for school districts regardless of source. School districts dependent on the state agencies express frustration over their relationship with them, and school districts dealing with developers, and others, likewise struggle for their fair share of funds.

Special combination plans. A number of districts have special combination plans for funding. The facilities planner for Monte Elementary School District had their most recently built school funded with state money in conjunction with the county's special education program. They are also acquiring developer and redevelopment fees.

The Dulce Unified School District is an example of a small school district with a limited but continuing building program. Because the district consists of small developers, the sources of funds are limited. The school district has attempted to acquire school sites rather than developer fees as part of the matching funds required for state allocation. Due to this community's high proportion of senior citizens who are not amenable to passing GOBs, the district has turned to Mello-Roos funds and redevelopment money.

Prairie Land, Bella Vista, Distant Place, Silent Spring, Wide Plains, Retreat, and Freeway View are school districts that have diligently sought other sources of funds after the state was unable to approve their applications. Their efforts in obtaining alternate funds have been unsuccessful. One of the facilities planners summed up their situation: "If you do not get the money, you get relocatables, and you survive until you can move ahead."

Facilities planners engage in decision making regarding the type of funding to be acquired, the actions necessary to acquire them, and the coordination of the relevant parties. Fiscal and legal experts provide technical assistance as professionals, and the representatives mobilize support. When any one or any combination of these factors falters, the fiscal plan is jeopardized.

Conclusions

The fiscal planning stage is problematic because the need for new facilities exceeds the available resources. The state provided the major portion of funds until it ran out of funds. School districts have been encouraged to seek alternative funding programs. School facilities planners have attempted to put together funding packages to complete their buildings. Some school districts have been able to combine state and other types of funding such as developer fees. Other school districts have used redevelopment for relocatables.

In general, the developer fees were helpful while development was taking place. The Mello-Roos community facilities districts have not been as beneficial as projected. GOBs have been difficult to pass and land banking has not been used by many of the districts in this sample. The common practice is to swap land with developers or others. The data do not show school districts seeking funds from the California School Finance Authority for the provision of alternative assistance for reconstructing, remodeling, replacing buildings, and acquiring new school sites or buildings.

Facilities planners maintain the executive function by leading and making the critical decisions in the process. Experts and professionals enter the process to provide technical, legal, and financial advice. The representatives vary the most in mobilizing support and limiting involvement, which highlights the linkage between facility need and source of funding.

The implications are that if school facilities are viewed as important public buildings, financial assistance should be sought from the federal government when the need is overwhelming, necessitating a rating of "disaster." When the need is created by new development, the local region should institute a system whereby the construction of the school facility is simultaneously carried out with the rest of the new development. The responsibility for this should be assumed by the area of growth and proportionately by the county, city, and district according to established benefit. When the need is created through population displacement, redevelopment and other types of funds should be available.

EDUCATIONAL SPECIFICATIONS DEVELOPMENT, SITE SELECTION, AND BUILDING DESIGN

The fourth step in the construction of school facilities includes three discrete activities: the development of educational specifications, site selection, and building design. Because the development of educational specifications and building design are so closely linked they will be discussed in one section, with a short section on the selection of the architect and another on site acquisition. The three activities are conducted simultaneously in order to avoid inconsistencies and build a school rather than just a facility. In this section, each of the activities will be treated within the process to demonstrate how they are integrated.

Activities interdependence

Cozy Corner Unified School District's facilities planner's description of this step demonstrates how the three activities are interwined:

> We have an architectural firm that has a demographic staff. We then go out to the community. We pull in members of the community to work with the architect and the staff to determine the educational specifications of our school. The architect then works on some basic designs.
>
> At present the district is at the preliminary stages regarding new site purchasing. We have selected a site, and an offer on the site will be given soon. The district plans to pay for the site with developer fees money.

The superintendent from Cozy Corner School District elaborated on the same process:

> You work with your architect and your staff to determine the best location for that school. If you do not have a site, you know someone owns that land, and you will have to buy it from them. And if it is already planned for houses and a school is not included, you may

have a conflict. The architect and I begin the process. And then we usually have a design committee that are volunteers. Most of them are teachers and administrators. We talk about what we need for the school, but we have a philosophy that drives our school designs. And that philosophy is based on a knowledge of how we think students learn. That becomes the foundation for our design. We consult with state officials who help us in the initial phase of selecting a school site. There are many people that you work with. And there is the architect and his staff, the state department people, and your community.

The successful execution of Step Four lies in the manner by which the three functions and activities are coordinated. The executive integrates the executive, professional, and representative functions and the three activities: development of educational specifications, building design, and selection of site. The degree to which the executive appreciates the interdependence of these three activities and the degree to which each function can be woven in will determine the smoothness of the process and the satisfaction with the facility after it is constructed.

Cozy Corner and Monte School Districts' facilities planners have taken the lead in orchestrating the three activities and providing a means for the professionals to participate. There are three major junctures where conflict can arise. The first is between the architectural and educational professionals. The facility's design may emphasize one over the other. The second is during the selection of the site, where the executive and representative functions may clash. The most desirable site may not be readily available from the community or affordable by the district. The third major juncture is between the executive and professionals. Architects may want to override executive wishes on the basis of their technical information regarding design.

Facilities planners act to avoid these junctures of conflict. One means is to hire a permanent architect to ensure constant interaction and loyalty to the district. A second one is to provide for the architect a defined role within the process. Finally, facilities planners attempt to retain their dominance over the entire process.

A description of the process demonstrates how the architect worked with the Cozy Corner Unified School District. The example provides instances where the architect's expertise holds the potential for assuming dominance over the process. Note how the architect draws parameters around his areas of responsibility:

In my work I do a lot of public buildings, schools, libraries, and that sort of thing. When working with schools, I deal with the superintendent and committees made up of teachers and principals and community members. It takes about seven meetings to develop the program which this school district would like to see. The members of the committee specify how many classrooms they want, if they want a multiuse area, or a performing arts area, or some other focus to the building. The square footage is determined from the number of students that it is going to serve. They get so many square feet per student. And then that determines the size of your school. You fit all of the program requirements within that square footage. There is a lot of give and take as you set up the program and begin the design of the project. You work with all of the consultants from the mechanical, electrical, structural, landscape, and civil areas. You put together a working package to approve the design. Then it is ready to bid. My preferred style for building design is contemporary. For this particular project, the client requested that the building look like a ranch house. Sixty thousand square feet are designed to pick up the contemporary character of a ranch house. Most of the time I like to let the project grow as people present their desires. The problem with architecture is that it is an art but you are restricted by many things: the expense of materials, the cost of the function of the building, and the mechanical and electrical requirements. In my practice, I work for the client, so I have to satisfy him or her. I do not design something that is not acceptable to the one who is paying for it; it becomes easier as your work is known because the districts know what to expect. Since my background is basically as a designer, I think I am usually better at creating an idea, developing it, and presenting it.

Compared to other school districts, Cozy Corner Unified School District successfully integrated its activities and functions; therefore, the district experienced few problem areas associated with design and educational specifications. The architect retained disciplined dominance over the various steps. He viewed himself working primarily for the superintendent and principal and then seeking approval from the board. He saw the process of the development of educational specifications and design requests in understanding the level—elementary, middle, or high school. Then he adhered to state standards as specified by each of the agencies. He knew he was limited to a certain square footage as related to level and that the classrooms and other types of areas had certain space and design requirements that had to be met. Third, he had budgetary and time constraints. The state budget allocations are strictly specified. There is more flexibility with other types of funding, but the district, nevertheless, imposes a budget to the design and a time schedule. Finally, the architect knew that educational and community representatives would have special requests:

We made the presentation to the school board directly because they are the ones who grant final approval. I designed and worked with the superintendent and principal and took it to be approved by the school board before we could proceed to the next step. Building new schools is political in the sense that you are working with political bodies like school board members. You may have three school board members that represent special interest groups. There are fights between teachers interested in education and teachers who want performing arts and theater areas. That is the political aspect. We solve problems like that by designing combination multiuse areas, which may include a library with sound walls for protection during a performance. We also stay within the allocated footage.

The data presented above show how interdependent the processes of developing educational specifications and building design are and how the architect plays a prominent role. The interplay between the various groups and the fluidity of the process is also demonstrated.

Educational specifications and building design

The most complete example regarding the development of educational specifications and building design is that followed by Hidden Springs Unified School District when Gypsy Elementary School was built. The principal from that elementary school explained how she participated in this step of the construction process:

> The design committee met weekly with the architect. There were representatives from the school board, district office personnel, classroom teachers, school secretaries, custodial staff, cafeteria staff, and parents. I was the principals' representative at that time, not knowing that I would be the principal of the school. Those who were involved in the design process comprised a comprehensive collection of people resulting in one of the most effective things that we could have done in order to come up with a school that so closely meets the needs of the kids.

The associate superintendent and facilities planner talked to the group and the architect; the architect then incorporated the ideas in the design. The process that Hidden Springs used to build Gypsy Elementary is that from the very beginning design stages, several years ago, everyone who had anything to do with an elementary school was involved and talking with the architect. The design committee met weekly with the architect. The architect presented an in-service workshop about the kinds of things you can and cannot do with school design. The members of the design committee visited other school sites and different types of schools in the surrounding area, including those that were basically all portable and those that were totally designed and constructed from the ground up. The principals and the teachers from those schools were interviewed about the positive and negative aspects of each school and how design details were incorporated. After an extensive deliberation period between the architect and the committee members, suggestions were incorporated by the architect to be part of Gypsy School.

Gypsy Elementary School today is a facility with the library as its focus. The principal's office is located with a view of the total campus. The students can study, individually or in groups, outside or inside classroom areas; stages, work spaces, and play stalls are available inside and outside the classrooms. The landscaping incorporates both students' activities and aesthetics. Parents are proud of an edifice that speaks for, and blends into, their neighborhood.

As stated above, most districts begin their educational specifications process by considering school level: elementary, middle, and high school. Architects are expected to know the design distinctions and requirements for each level. An understanding of the basic design requirements provide for the architect a point of departure for the rest of the considerations of the educational specifications for the building.

An assurance that the architect has an understanding of the school plant construction is best obtained when the principal of the school is involved from the beginning, as was the case with Hidden Springs. However, sometimes even when principals participate actively, they later discover that the architect failed to include critical elements in the design. For example, a principal of one of one of the elementary schools of the University Unified School District cited this experience with his school:

> The thing that I am finding now is that the architect should have submitted to the committee a list of things that we would want or not want in the school rather than have the committee report to us because the people on the committee were lay people, who did not know a lot of things, and I find that I assumed a lot of things to be part of the school that are not. As an example, in the last week, I discovered that they did not include a safe in the office. The reaction is, "Oh, schools do not have safes." But that is not true. All schools have safes. Last Friday I was running around trying to buy a safe because they were pouring concrete in the office. I was unable to get it so the supervisor blocked out a hole in the concrete so I can have a safe later on. Another example was to have a place for a kiln. All elementary schools have

kilns. So that is something we are going to have to add. Drinking fountains were not designed in any of the classrooms. Sinks were in, but without faucets. It is things like that, I would think, an architect who designs schools would know are part of an elementary school, but we are finding that those things were not included in our school. My worry is that if we are identifying these things now, what will we find once we move in? I feel badly about it because 4 million dollars have been spent for this school and it is not perfect. The drawback is that the architect had something in mind for a new school, and the committee had something different. I am feeling more and more that we are getting a school that we did not ask for. Architecturally, the aesthetics, the design, the elevations of the school are not exactly what we asked for. We wanted a Spanish Mediterranean style to fit into the community, but what we have is a modern school with a red tile roof.

As can be seen from the above, Green Wash Elementary School had several problems with its design. The architect explained that one reason the Spanish Mediterranean style was not incorporated was because the district changed architects in the middle of the process and he was never told that the district wanted arched windows rather than gabled. Also, the inexperience of the district in constructing schools led to some misunderstandings and unfulfilled expectations. The architect said,

University has not built a new building in 15-20 years so virtually nobody there really knows how to build a school. They have not experienced it. So one of the main problems we have had is actually educating them on how the process is going. My boss has had to go over there and speak with them about how the process works. Not to get too uptight about words like "change orders" and "revisions." I have worked with clients that have done so much building that we literally just hand them over the plans and they take it from there. They handle the bids, the construction, and do everything because they know what they are doing.

University, thus, demonstrates how a school may be built with many extra nice things, but may lack important elements associated with schooling. It may also be built in a different style from that expected. But what is most clearly demonstrated in this case is the manner in which the functions were faulty. The executive's function erred due to the lack of experience and being unable to integrate the educational specifications within the building design. The professional's function erred when the principal was unable to affect the design and the architect failed to integrate the district's wishes. The representative's function erred through their limited participation.

Most of the CERC member school districts followed a similar process in the selection of the design for their schools. They had an advisory group consisting of representatives from the community, school board, school district, and the architect. They visited schools they thought would represent the types of schools they would consider. They would select a general type and begin to develop the educational specifications, usually based on a general philosophical statement presented by the superintendent. Some school districts used their printed philosophical statement to guide them in their deliberations. The focus of the school was then linked to the philosophical statement. For example, Hidden Springs interpreted their philosophy to mean that the library is the most important room in the building, and that everything should radiate from there. Other schools viewed multiuse rooms, theater, gymnasium, science laboratories, and the administrative offices as their focus for the design of their schools.

The elementary schools are the most common and numerous being built. There are some middle schools and a few high schools being built. Elementary schools' concerns are their classrooms, whereas middle schools' concerns are science and computer laboratories. High schools' concerns center on the disciplines, for example, sciences versus humanities and the arts. Aside from Hidden Springs, most architects appear to prefer that educational specifications be developed among school and community representatives and then receive them from the school administrators. Few schools are built with such an extensive, consultative process as that undergone by Hidden Springs. And even in this district, the elementary school built after Gypsy used the Gypsy plan rather than attempt to design a new one from the start.

After the general type of facility has been decided upon and the educational specifications have been developed, the architect is then usually presented with a specific style. This is important because every school being built must incorporate at least a third of its area in relocatables, and the building's style may be affected. Architects tend to originate their own style and incorporate the community's requirements and wishes. Some communities, however, such as University, have definite ideas about the types of buildings they want in their neighborhoods. University's experience demonstrates how the district's style preference can be ignored and a beautiful contemporary school can be built rather than what was requested.

Two school districts have selected one style (cookie cutter) for all of their elementary schools. One school district's architect has asked that the district change the style because their firm is tired of building the same type of facility. One school district's facilities planner worked closely and individually with the architect to incorporate the educational specifications in the building design for all of the district's schools. Some school districts' elementary schools consist totally of relocatables.

Identical designs for middle and high schools are less likely: first, because sites are seldom amenable; and second, neighborhoods, faculties, and students differ across the district. Most importantly, middle and high schools are not built in sufficient numbers within a district to enable duplication, and districts and architects apparently don't swap plans.

Several conditions determine the extent to which educational specifications can be met. "Schools for the twenty-first century" means new technology needs, but these are currently not included in the state's requirements. Wiring, fiber optics, microwave, computers, or other technologies are not being incorporated into state requirements for school construction (see MacConnell and Associates, 1989). Thus, schools being built now may not be adequate for the twenty-first century, and even though educational professionals may request technical educational specifications, the state may be unprepared to approve them.

Fiscal conditions also serve to determine the extent to which educational specifications can be met. Elementary and middle schools' science and computer laboratory needs are seldom met. Secondary schools are seldom able to fully incorporate all disciplines.

Regulatory conditions regarding space and access allocations also affect decisions regarding the fulfillment of educational specifications. State regulations regarding size, safety, and supervision constrain school design. School personnel, such as teachers, may also object to certain educational specifications resulting in limited building designs. Daisy Middle School in the Cozy Corner Unified School District is an example of a facility in which these conditions interacted in the process.

The science teacher from Cozy Corner described how the design of their school was affected by the various conditions:

> Every classroom had to be able to function for every subject area. The science lab would be shared by three grades: sixth, seventh, and eighth. Another part of the design is that this school is an open school all under one roof, with most of the classrooms open. We had been polled as an entire faculty on that prior to the four or five of us going

to the community in order to approve that design. One teacher is not teaching in this middle school because she did not want to be in an atmosphere where her room would be open for public view. She did not want to teach behind a glass door.

School districts and architects work best when the executive integrates these activities, when the professionals remain within their area of specialization, and when representatives are able to express their preferences. For the school district, an important part of this process is to have the right person as the architect.

The selection of the architect

As has been shown from the data presented above, one reason the architect assumes dominance is because school districts' facilities planners do not have experience in building schools. Another reason is because architects become integrated within the school district's social system. The architect is then trusted to make the best decisions for the school district. Conversely, the executive can retain dominance over this process if the architect participates meaningfully within his jurisdication. School districts, thus, select architects to assist them comprehensively as they build their schools. The board president from Cozy Corner Unified School District said, "The district hired an architectural firm to assist us in statistical gathering and understanding the state process in the construction of the schools beginning with the design phase."

Cactus Ranch Unified School District is illustrative of the types of relationships school districts develop with their architects. The facilities planner related, "You have to find an architect to help you get the building built. Our architects are a local firm. We drive past their offices every day, so we can drop things off, and there is a feeling that they represent the district as well as work for it." Silent Spring Unified School District, likewise, placed great trust in the work and diligence of their architect of many years. The architect not only concerned himself with the design of the facilities but monitored the district's construction progress.

Retreat Unified School District used two architects to build their new schools. One agency designed their elementary schools while the other designed their secondary ones.

Sometimes, the district and the architects are unable to work together. Several school districts changed architects during the data gathering period. Green Valley Unified School District, for example, replaced their architect because he was very slow and his ideas were not useful to them. The board wanted him to fly up to Sacramento to stay there and work out problems until resolved, whereas he wanted to meet with everyone and talk things out. The new architect was selected by board members, who considered his track record, design style, and whether he had had problems. School districts are most satisfied with architects who are involved throughout the construction process.

Site acquisition

Site acquisition is handled by school districts in different ways depending on how the need for a new school is perceived. When the developer and school district agree there is a need for new schools, sites may be readily provided within the development area. If the school growth is related to scattered developments or displacement, the district may or may not have desirable sites. If the district does not have at least three sites from which to choose, the district needs to locate sites in order to initiate application for new construction state funds, and submit for state approval. The state inspects the three sites and finally approves one.

Site acquisition is problematic because it has to meet state mandated environmental impact standards, soil and other ground requirements, and must not exceed 10 percent of the total facility cost. Many school districts decide on school-level need (elementary, middle, or senior high schools) and then search for adequate acreage. While that is taking place, the architect and educational professionals work on the design of the school and the needs for the site. The budget for the entire facility can then be determined and the purchase of the site may be facilitated.

School districts' sites differ widely in their needs. Some school districts don't have land available. Others have a difficult time purchasing land for their schools, and a few swap land. Many school districts have land with particular problems. The architect for Cozy Corner Unified School District, for example, explained,

> This site had particular problems because it is hilly. We had to reduce the size of the site and flatten it. The most economical way to build schools is to have flat sites. That way, the state does not have to pay for drainage systems. It is expensive to cut slopes, remove dirt, put drainage systems, and that sort of thing. In this region there aren't that many flat sites available for schools. Now the housing developers set aside a school site. There are certain requirements and guidelines for a site. An elementary school requires 10 acres, a

middle school 18-20 acres, and a high school 40 acres to define the site. Once the site is selected, the program and design process begins.

In contrast, University Unified School district had a different problem. The board president explained it this way: "In University when we want to buy a site, we consider the location. For example, our high school site is a controversial thing because no one wants to have it anywhere. It is difficult because you want to build it where there is a demand but the community does not want it."

Hanging Bridge Unified School District's problem is that the desirable land is residential property. The school district is not able to purchase homes because it cannot provide the homeowners with enough money to relocate. Home purchasing takes place only when a few homes are located on ideal school sites. Hanging Bridge, which was once known for its citrus groves, is now a city with only one grove remaining. Although the grove would be an ideal site for a new school, the facilities planner does not want to be known as the man who eradicated the last citrus grove in the city.

In brief, Marica, Retreat, and Silent Spring School Districts cannot afford to purchase land.

Cactus Ranch Unified School District's facilities planner summarized, "Once you determine that you need a school and where the growth is occurring, you try to acquire a site. There is a lot that takes place. The environmental impact study gives you permission from the state to pay for the site."

Dry Lake Unified School District explained how the state becomes involved in this activity: "Site selection is determined by the local board of trustees, but CSDE/SFPD plays a major role in the site selection through its field representative that comes out to the local school district and approves the site for the particular school." The district had an advisory group in the site selection of the high school. CSDE/SFPD became involved in the suitability and location of the school site for educational purposes. It determined if the site was acceptable by examining proximity to freeways, airports, industry, and land slopes. Although the land developers had suggestions, the last word was that of CSDE/SFPD.

Conclusions

During this step, facilities planners need to be mindful of integrating and coordinating the many actors involved in the design of the facility, the selection of the site, and the incorporation of the educational specifications. The educational specifications are drawn from the state standards and regulations and the school district's educational philosophy. The building's design is drawn from the community's preferences and the architect's aesthetic value and competence. Integrating all of these aspects is important in the successful execution of this step. The architect is critical in developing the design and the principal is important in determining the educational specifications that are essential for the particular facility. Facilities planners must also acquire the proper site for the building. The executive must orchestrate the actors and activities within the district and facilitate the progress of the process by interacting positively with the state agencies.

The development of the educational specifications, building design, and site acquisition are the three activities that must be carried out simultaneously in order to ensure that the facility under construction results in a schoolhouse. This phase is problematic because the executive's responsibility is to integrate the three activities and coordinate the professional and representative functions. The integration of the educational specifications within the building design is jeopardized when the educational and architectural professionals are not coordinated in their activities. The coordination is most likely to occur through a lengthy and intense working relationship between the two, as illustrated in the case of Gypsy Elementary School from the Hidden Springs Unified School District. The process breaks apart—first, because school districts are inexperienced in the process. As the facilities planner from Green Valley explained, "We built no schools for twenty years, and now we are talking about opening two schools this year and two more next year and are projected to have twenty-seven schools within seven years to house twelve thousand students when we unify." Most of the school districts' facilities planners were not experienced and, likewise, architects were not experienced in constructing schools. Their professional activities had been in other areas. An exception to this was the architectural firm retained by Cactus Ranch Unified School District. In general, however, most school districts had to hire architects who were not specialists in building schools. Sometimes school districts hired two architects, one who specialized in elementary schools and another who specialized in secondary schools. The lack of experience at the district level and in architectural firms meant that many school districts changed architects over the course of the building process.

A second place where the process is jeopardized is when the executive fails to provide adequate opportunities for the architect to obtain the educational specifications from the professionals or educators, and the desires and expectations from the representatives or community. University Unified School District, for example, shows how the inexperienced facilities planner wished she knew more about what teachers need in their classrooms. The principal, likewise, was disappointed in the architect's limited knowledge regarding the provision of sink and fountain facilities, a safe, a kiln, and other details. The architect was defensive because he was brought into the process after most of the school design had been drawn, and a review of that design was never conducted to ensure congruence in expectations. Instead, the architect integrated the educational specifications he understood into a style he preferred. In this case, both professionals and activities were not coordinated by the executive. The representatives were also limited in their participation during this step. In summary, the executive's primacy during this phase cannot be underestimated. The integration of the activities and coordination of the relevant parties are critical to success.

Site acquisition is portrayed in the literature as requiring committee and advisory group input, but the data for this report indicate that the social and current conditions mitigate against much exchange. First, the available land, the need to construct schools in rapid succession, and the state's requirements for eligibility constrain the school district's latitude in engaging too many parties. The typical practice is to identify three sites, conduct the environmental impact study, have the state department examine the proposed sites, and have one approved. Including the site as part of the educational specifications and building design is difficult to integrate into the total process. The usual pattern is to have the architect adapt the design to the site rather than identify a site that is consistent with the educational specifications and building design.

A review of the reorganization and adaptation of the school district to its project—building schools—shows that school districts reorganize on an ad hoc basis as the process moves along. Instead of creating a unit responsible for the construction of schools, school personnel move in and out to execute the required tasks. For example, project management calls for a permanent executive. In the cases cited above, many school districts had several persons assuming the executive role, even though they may have appointed a facilities planner.

Project management also calls for the coordination and integration of internal and external parties. The process of constructing educational facilities calls for professionals and representatives at various junctures. The absence of these actors is related to the ambiguous structure of the project. The executive function is not consistently enacted by the facilities planner. The professionals and representatives do not assume responsibility for the project, such as in the GOB campaign for University City. School districts, thus, illustrate how a project is accomplished with ad hoc reorganization and continuous adaptation to the requirements of the process.

Chapter 4

The Construction of New Schools

BIDDING AND CONTRACTING

After the school design has been developed, the project is ready for bidding. The bidding process is described by the contractor for the Cozy Corner School District:

> I go about submitting a bid by giving office plans to the generals and they let them out to different subcontractors: mechanical, plumbing, and electrical. These people look at them, phone in bids to my company. All of the separate bids go into one big bid that is opened on bidding day. There is a lot of competition in the bidding process. On this job, for example, there were seven general contractors and fifteen different trades involved. In formulating a bid, our company has an extensive computer system that punches in man hours, specific areas, previous costs, and current projected costs. When we are in the bidding process, we know that number (parameter of the bid) and when somebody else bids we match their number to ours. Usually, the bids are close and we have to make split decisions which way to go. We consider quality, the subs that are connected, and our profit margin. We bid this school at $5,700,000.

Several contractors bid on school projects. Public work is usually granted to the lowest bidder. Sometimes she or he is not the best contractor. For the architect, it is important that the working drawings are comprehended by the contractor. Architects normally monitor the construction process. The school board president of Cozy Corner explained that the school district could have several contractors working on the various schools.

The facilities planner from the University Unified School District explained that the application of standard contract language by their attorney approves part of the bid. The architect and purchasing director put together the specifications. She said,

> I am not really involved in the bidding. You see, we plan the school and the architect and purchasing get together and they make sure that it is advertised and posted or whatever they have to do to make sure that all the construction companies know about it. They schedule the opening of the bids. Sometimes you have a site visit, but I don't know if we had one on this project. Either they are required to visit the site or sometimes we have a pre-bid conference where people interested in bidding on the job come meet with the architect and look at the place and answer many questions, which sometimes is required in order to bid.

Most elementary school projects are a one-year job from start to finish. The architect from Green Valley School District described going to bid:

> I don't have any contact with the contractor regarding design and style of the buildings until it is time to bid the project. Then we have a very normal public bid process and a number of contractors in that area, local players, those qualified to do school work, participate. You have to be a big reputable contractor to do school work. And so there are several local firms that bid every project and for each project you get a few guys who try to get in and that is kind of scary. You hope you do not get one of those, even though that sounds bad. But if they have done school work before and they know the process, it can go through much easier and the project is built faster and better and we make more money on it.

Pre-bid conference

The bidding process requires two distinct activities. The first is the pre-bid conference to establish a responsible contractor and the second is the actual bidding meeting. The literature and school districts are ambivalent about the function of the pre-bid conference. Some school districts are advised by their attorneys against them because some contractors may benefit over others. The pre-bid conference is of special importance to the architect, who assumes responsibility from the design phase through construction. Those districts whose architects' participation is limited in the construction are likely to have a construction manager hired to oversee the construction project. Construction managers may be hired without going to bid.

Architects prefer to monitor the construction process and they tend to request a pre-bid conference with contractors in order to determine "responsible contractors" or eligible contractors. One of the architects from one of the districts that hired construction managers and did not hold a pre-bid conference referred to the experience as one where he learned "if the contractor starts asking questions after the bid has been awarded, you know you're in trouble." What he meant is that a responsible contractor will seek details and specifics concerning the project to be bid. The one person with that information is the architect. The conference interaction provides the occasion for the architect to determine whether the contractor can build a school, and, thereby, prequalify bidders. Another advantage to the pre-bid conference is the determination of subletting. Attorneys and architects sometimes differ over the usefulness of a pre-bid conference.

Bidding meeting

The second activity is the bidding meeting itself. The process is highly regulated and standardized. The bids are let out in an established procedure specifying board meeting, date and time, and room. One staff member is made responsible for handling the bidders. Telephones are available and bidders' requests are anticipated. All bids are to be opened at a specific time and all clocks are synchronized. Sealed bids are noted and the opening of the bids is official. Some of these practices appear trivial, but they are important and help to avoid legal and technical problems. The bids are opened, names are provided, the amount is specified, and the completeness of the package is acknowledged. A written acknowledgment addendum is filed to avoid disputes. The bids, including the listing of all subcontractors, are read. All documents are saved, duplicated, and meticulously filed. If all bids are above the anticipated one, bidders are informed and the board may be advised to reject all bidders.

Irregularities below bid require additional study. Everything is recorded in words and numbers. Legal counsel is sought as necessary. Split bids are not advised. All of these procedures, and limits and advertising for materials and work, are required by law. When bids are not awarded the public is informed and all bids are public information. A letter specifying the conditions for the award of the bid is provided. Lowest bidder is rejected if the bidder is not responsible. "Responsible" is defined "as the bidder that can do the job." Bids are considered "non-responsible" when forms are not completed properly. The rejected lowest bidder is granted due process. The issue of letting, holding, or releasing bidders is specified.

Subcontractors are protected on the major contract. The specification of the architect as providing follow-up services and monitoring the construction is included. California requires that the Subletting and Fair Practices Act be employed throughout the subletting process. These subcontractors file their bids for the job within the last 2-3 hours on the filing day by phoning or faxing in to the contractor. Accordingly, he must analyze these quickly for correctness and price and then list these subcontractors by name in his bid to the architect. This is peculiar to public-work contracting and can be problematic if the contractor or architect is not familiar with the subcontractors' work quality.

The construction of educational facilities is clearly within the purview of the state legislatures. Generally, this state responsibility is delegated to the local school district. Construction management (CM) is utilized when a district engages a firm to coordinate a total project with the objective of representing the district's best interests. The CM firm is responsible for exercising highly skilled professional judgment and possessing technical expertise in such areas as material design and selection, cost estimates and budgets, schedules and coordination, supervision of construction, and certification of contractor payments. The typical contractual relationship between the school board and the CM firm is similar to that with the architect/engineer. As a general rule, contracts for personal or professional services by a public body with a private firm or individual are not governed by public competitive bidding. California utilizes construction management without bids. The data for this study included a school district that hired a CM connected to a construction firm. His work on the school facility was described as a disaster by the school board president. There are several reasons why the CM was not successful. First, the firm was granted a high degree of independence. Second, since it did not have to bid, a record of its competence was not made public. Third, because it was an outside firm, it did not become integrated into the school system, leading to a neglect to incorporate educational specifications. In sum, the construction process was not successful because the state agencies and school district's facilities planner abdicated their responsibility while the construction management firm worked independently.

Contracting

The bidding process is problematic because it is competitive. Several factors interact in this competition. First, since school facility construction was not common when the need for school construction became necessary, very few contractors could qualify to bid. However, as the need for new schools increased, more and more contractors entered the process. As the economic cycle evolved, some school districts had school facility construction approval and funds, whereas new development was decreasing. For many construction firms, this meant a new area to enter. For some school districts' communities, this was one of the highest employment areas, so many firms competed in the bid.

During the bidding and contracting step, the architect is responsible for adherence to the design; it is therefore in his interest to have the bid awarded to the best contractor. But for public works, the award is to the lowest bid: many contractors bid low to get the project; others, due to inexperience. The architect strives to have the project go to a reputable and dependable contractor. The data in this study show that the greater the interdependence between the architect and the contractor, the greater the likelihood that the architect's design will prevail. Many of the problems associated with construction can be avoided if they are considered during the pre-bid conference and if the bidding process includes active participation by the architect to determine whether the contractors can be relied upon to adhere to the design.

The bidding process includes the active participation of the facilities planner, the architect, and the attorney. Some school districts call for consultants from the state to ensure that the bid contract meets the state requirements. Some consultants serve as inspectors, from the bid through the construction process. If the architect is experienced, the architect prepares the bid and bid process to ensure that contractors are informed about the process and the construction requirements. Sometimes general contractors are given approximately four weeks to study forthcoming projects. The pre-bid conference is held during this period, and interaction between contractors and architects can determine the contractor's eligibility and compatibility. Another advantage to the pre-bid conference is that the contractor can determine what kinds of subletting will be permitted.

The costs for school construction projects are fairly predictable. The prevailing wages and the costs for materials and equipment are set. The price for contractors came down 20 percent during the course of the study. School districts caught during the downturn period have discovered that the low bids can create difficulties. The margin between bids is very small, but if the lowest bid comes from inexperienced or out-of-contracts contractors, the district may be in for trouble.

The executive function during this step is to authorize the bid and bidding process. The professional function is fulfilled by the architect and the attorney. The attorney ensures that the procedure is proper and that the legal documents and contracts are in order. The architect is the critical actor because he is in the position to draw up the bid with enough detail to disqualify incompetent contractors. The representative function legitimizes the total process. The conflicts that arise during this period are related to the dominance of the architect, the architect's inexperience, and the contractor's incompetence.

The data show a school district whose facilities planner and architect relinquished the responsibilities to an inspector, who monitored the provision of all of the state requirements but failed to account for many other details specific to schools. The superintendent and board of education had a lot of explaining to do and the construction of the next school facility was jeopardized. When the school building is found to be faulty, both the executive and representative functions enter the process defensively.

Sometimes the legal requirements for the bidding process intimidate both architect and contractors from exchanging the critical information and from assessing each other's competencies. The superintendent and school board are also excluded from the process by law.

Conclusions

This step is best conducted when a pre-bid conference is provided, when the architectural firm is experienced, and when the contractor specializes in school building construction. The use of subcontractors under the general contractor for the total project appears to provide a better means for coordination than the provision of independent subcontractors. However, the data for this report show that it is the assurance that contractors and subcontractors are familiar with school buildings and that a good working relationship exists between the architect and the contractor that leads to a well-designed and well-built facility. The provision of these conditions occurs during the bidding process. Thus, part of the facilities planner's responsibility is to see that this activity takes place.

One reason facilities planners are reticent to participate in a pre-bid conference is because during this informing activity, some contractors may benefit more than others. The legal, professional, and social interpretations concerning the nature of the activity vary. For example, the activity may turn out to be a marketing opportunity for the contractor rather than a mutual exchange of information regarding the building design. Another observation is that the activity may involve a larger group of persons than can adequately discuss the critical dimensions of the project. Assessing and informing do not take place.

The consequences of a faulty bidding process are shown by the data to be (1) the necessity to hire a manager to oversee the total project because the architect and general contractor can't work together; (2) the necessity to call in an inspector to ensure that all state requirements and standards are met; and (3) additional expenses related to changes and errors in the construction.

It is recommended that the bidding process be viewed as more than a legal and technical process. An understanding of the social and competitive nature of the process necessitates the institutionalization of an informing and assessing activity—the pre-bid conference—between the architect, contractor, and school executive. The facilities planner should oversee the two parts to the bidding step. The school board, serving the representative function, should be integrated into the process to ensure that eligibility to bid to build a school facility is determined prior to the bidding. The contract awarded will, therefore, be more likely to satisfy state requirements, the school district, and its community.

FACILITY CONSTRUCTION

After the bidding process has been completed, the project is ready for construction. The groundbreaking ceremony begins the construction phase. The contractor for Cozy Corner Unified School District described his participation:

> I was a part of the groundbreaking ceremony. It is basically to introduce everybody that is involved in the project. At this one we had the superintendent of schools, the principal, the architect, a couple of secretaries, and me. That was the first time that all of us gathered as a unit. We just introduced ourselves and the superintendent just stuck the golden shovel into the ground, had her picture taken, and it was over.

Groundbreaking

Groundbreaking is a ceremonial part of the construction process. It is an important activity because it informs the public that the school is going to be built and it introduces the construction company to the community. The community is assured its funds are well-spent, and it is prepared for any inconveniences the construction may cause. Even though very few from the community attend this event, acknowledging it publicly alerts people that the school is being built.

From our sample of school districts, many school districts failed to hold groundbreaking ceremonies and one of them, University Unified School District, felt holding the event would be problematic. The facilities planner for University offered an explanation regarding the beginning stages of construction of the new school:

> The school was built in two phases. Site work was done first and then relocatables were moved on to the property. The school consisting of relocatables is open as a temporary site while the other half of the campus is under construction. It is hard to say exactly when construction on the school itself began. When should you schedule a groundbreaking ceremony? The decision to withhold the groundbreaking ceremony was based on the fact that we recently failed two bond issues asking for funds for three new schools. In light of this, we did not want to advertise that we had the funds to build a new school. This decision was an administrative decision. You must realize that this is the first school to open in 20-30 years in this district and the first for me. I am perhaps ignorant of the significance of the ceremony.

The construction of Green Wash Elementary School thus began without public acknowledgment. Children were housed in the Green Wash School site in relocatables while the school facility was being constructed. The students subsequently would move to the facility when completed and the relocatables would be moved or used while another school would be under construction.

What is to be noted in the case of University is that if the construction process is disrupted at any one step, the repercussions are carried on to the subsequent ones. Because the community of University had not supported the construction of additional schools two bond issues had failed and the district built Green Wash Elementary School without a groundbreaking ceremony, the construction of the school was disrupted and unsatisfactory.

Changes

There are several important considerations during the construction phase. First, the architect's design is to be followed. Second, there are budget and time limitations. Third, the process is expected to be a smooth one.

Because the growth in the area being studied has been so rapid and funds for schools unavailable, many school districts have applied creative ways of housing their students while construction was going on. The construction phase was one of excitement and anticipation, and those involved voiced their particular concerns.

The principal from Gypsy Elementary School in the Hidden Springs Unified School District put it this way:

> As a principal I would spend more time on the construction site because many of the little things we have seen that need to be changed are because we did not see them during the construction process. An example of that is the one wall in my office that has no electrical outlets. It is critical for the computer, the printer, and those sorts of things. A construction crew has no idea what goes on in a principal's office. If I had been on site more, I would have noticed those details and would have been able to take care of those early on.

The superintendent of Cozy Corner Unified School District voiced this concern:

> During construction what you want to do is reduce changes with the design. It is very difficult because once that school is designed and approved, and you make a major change, you have to go through a whole different approval process. You can have a minor change order and make an adjustment with that, but it is important to be sure you know what you want in the beginning as a global plan, because if not, you may delay your project.

The architect at Cozy Corner described how changes affect the construction stage.

> We are changing things right now as it is under construction. It is more costly because it is a change from the original contract but you can still make changes while under construction. If it is already finished you could still make a change but it is going to be even more difficult. So, the idea is that if changes are necessary they be during this time so it does not stop construction. We did not design the middle school with a sophisticated science lab area. Now we are going back and putting chemical-proof tops and upgrading. The problem is that the slab and plumbing are already in. We had to go back and cut out the slab and the contractor loses momentum because he has to take a step backwards instead of going forward. He has to go back and work on an area which he could have finished before. So it is kind of a hindrance. But we do make changes up to the very end. And that is processed through change orders.

In order to avoid difficulties with changes, the architect and contractor develop a working style among themselves. The architect explained:

> Our firm holds weekly job meetings on the site. We have a guy in our office that is a field administrator that attends those meetings. The project architect, like myself, oversees the whole project and if there are problems I need to get involved with, I will be involved with them. So, on a weekly basis we meet with the contractor on site. If I come across a flaw in the design prior to construction, I notify the contractor. Everybody concerned gets informed because it involves money and additional expenditures. I have an inspector who is supposed to be informed if there is a problem, but I have to correct a design flaw through the contractor because it may or may not increase the cost. The inspector bids on the project. If it is within a reasonable fixing range it may not cost anything, but if it is not, it may increase the cost which I have to approve.

The contractor and architect, therefore, work to be sure changes are handled in a professional manner and meet all state requirements. The changes usually affect others besides the architect and contractor, and changes may be due to many factors, including oversights or errors by the state agencies. The principal from Daisy Middle School explained why the science labs required a change: "The only difficulty that we have encountered in having the facility under construction is the state changed the guidelines for science labs. Therefore, we had to go back and make some changes in the science lab area in the building. And that is the only problem we have had."

The contractor from Cozy Corner, relating an oversight by OSA, said, "Or perhaps the OSA structural engineer will come out and suddenly realize, 'Well, we did not look at things closely enough, so we have a major problem here.' Typically, OLA could pay for something like that."

An example of a change that is required because the contractor and architect read the design differently is described by the contractor for Cozy Corner:

> There are areas where, in some of the little rooms that are for mechanical storage, there is not quite enough room for the equipment that they want to put there. So, you have to move the wall a little bit. Mostly, it is a clarification of what the architect is trying to get at because it is hard to cover every detail on a set of prints.

When changes require sub-contractors and state approval, the contractor assumes dominance in the process to ensure that all technical and legal requirements are fulfilled. The contractor from University explained how he handles major change orders:

The contractor would go to the sub involved and get a price for the change order. He would apply a profit and return it to the architect. The architect would review this with his consultants and would generate an official job-change order. This would be sent to all parties, owner through general contractor, for signature. This finally would be sent to the state for approval. Then it would become a real job-change order, and the contractor could bill it. This process would normally take a month to complete. However, if the change is one which will likely hold up the project, the contractor may proceed with a change, providing a written authorization pending a future change order from the owner and the architect, is provided.

Many times, the specifics of the building are not fully appreciated or understood by the contractors, so architects and school districts include a "grandfather clause" to protect them in case contractors don't adhere strictly to the building codes. The contractor from University explained:

> As a way to protect the architect from financial responsibilities, contracts often include "grandfather clauses." Those clauses necessitate the contractor to apply building codes and construction laws regardless of the quality of the set of drawings which were intended to reflect them.

Sometimes school districts hire a state inspector to ensure that all state regulations and standards are met. The data indicate that an inspector is not necessary when school facilities are being built by experienced architects and contractors. The data also show that even with state inspectors, the state requirements may be minimally fulfilled but the quality of the facility may be compromised.

The executive function is overall supervision, and the professionals—architect and contractor—likewise provide the necessary technical supervision. When the school district's executive does not specify the role of the architect as a professional supervisor in the process, the contractor may compromise his role as well. Technically and legally this occurs through the hiring of a construction manager. Another actor who moves into the process is the state inspector. The state inspector fulfills his or her role effectively by ensuring that all state regulations and standards are met, but he or she relinquishes all areas relating to quality of materials and workmanship to the contractor or architect.

The problems arising from the above begin with change orders. The architect for Green Valley Unified School District related his experiences with a particular contractor:

Building a facility is constant trouble. The changes, and wanting to get paid for changes, has been problematic for us. Because you are on a fixed budget, whether it be local or state funded, there is not an endless pocket for change orders. So what we try to do when things come up is that we try to save money somewhere else on the project later on so we can balance those things. That's a real trick, trying to keep the project at the bid amount through the whole construction phase without the contractor being allowed a lot of money for change orders.

Sometimes changes have to be made when the building is almost completed. For example, Green Valley had to have a door added at Bended Creek Elementary School. The architect elaborated:

We wanted to be sure there was a door between the computer lab and the multipurpose room so there would be access without having to go through a classroom to get to the computer lab. So there was a need to have a change order, and we took that to the board and they approved it. We are all very happy that happened. It made access to the lab easier for everybody in the whole school.

Aside from the inconveniences and expenses involved with changes, the school district, the architect, and the contractor need to be concerned about state approval for the changes. The architect explained:

One of the things that we always do if a change requires state school building funds or if it is a change we feel is going to need approval from funding sources, like the OLA or the SAB, is to get written approval from them, before we initiate any change. Districts who do not go through that process may very likely have those agencies say, "We did not approve it," and be stuck with those bills. If districts move forward with the changes without the approvals, they may find not only conflict, but opposition to the changes and may find themselves in a position to make payments they had not anticipated. You also might find your contractor not willing to take the risk without approvals from the proper agencies.

Architect and contractor relationships

Changes affect the relationship between the architect and the contractor as shown in the Green Valley case. But the day-to-day work also contributes to straining relationships. Both professionals have to strive for an amiable relationship.

The general contractor for Cozy Corner explained how he views construction taking place.

A smooth building process is dependent upon cooperation among the trades. Attitudes, cooperation with the school district, the architect, and whether the plans on specifications are clear and thorough need to be worked on. So far we have not had major problems. It has all been small stuff, which is true in every job. You are trying to do a three dimensional job from one dimensional subprints. It is hard to do without having some glitches here and there.

In striving for a positive working relationship, the contractor and the architect respect each other's areas of responsibility, even when one does not understand the other's view. For example in the case of Daisy Middle School, the contractor and the architect do not perceive the facility's style in the same way. Nevertheless, the contractor builds to the architect's specifications. The contractor for Daisy Middle School explained:

I know the faculty is going to enjoy this school because it has some unique ideas. It is not just a flat-top roof. It is supposed to look like a ranch. That was the original concept: that the building blend with the community. However, it really is not looking like a ranch. That is the only concept idea that I am having a little bit of trouble with, but I think that it is going to fit into the surroundings alright.

The Cozy Corner contractor provides an example of the way the professionals, architect and contractor, establish their areas of jurisdiction. In this way the school facility gets built smoothly.

During the construction phase, a critical part is to adhere to the time limits. The contractor from Cozy Corner put it this way:

We have to complete this building for the amount under contract. We have to build it for $5, 700,000 and we have to do it in fourteen months. If we run behind we are up for a lawsuit. Or we are up for penalties. The penalties range from job to job. They could be $500 a day to $2,000 a day. It depends on many things. We do not get penalized when we get behind because of somebody else's delay, if it is justifiable, or if we took more time to make requested changes, or added to the project little things here and there. We also get extra days for contingencies. When we originally signed the contract we had fourteen months and now that has been extended by whatever rains we have had. That gets added in so we keep extending the contract and it does not help us. We also shut down when it is windy.

One of the architects, who first started with his father, related that school construction has remained the same. There are no new designs nor technologies that are radically different from those applied two decades ago. Some schools use a model set of plans. Some engineering and structural aspects have been refined, and most school districts build different schools throughout the district, but the fundamental elements regarding schools have not changed. Playgrounds are simple and typically include an asphalt area and a grassy field. The classroom interiors remain similar. They are thirty square feet, with dropped lighting and some windows. Colors vary. Carpets are typically glued down. New technology, high voltage, lasers, and optical disks are rare in school buildings. Everyone is using air conditioning now. Building tends to be cyclical. All of these jobs are bid and extremely competitive, so it pays to be a dependable, established architect in order to rely on a long-time record.

When the construction management system is used by school districts, the school district acts as owner/builder. The contractor acts and advises in the planning and building phase. Educators make their requests known, and the contractor guides them through the process. Architects are called in as consultants and hire engineers to handle the technical problems.

Conclusions

The construction process consists of two major activities: the preparation of the site and the actual construction of the building. The construction of the building is based on the architect's design. Presumably, for schools, the design would have been formulated by educators and architects. Contractors use these designs to construct the building.

Contractors are structured in three basic ways. The first is that the general contractor bids on the total project and is part of a company that can provide all of the associated services. Few general contractors assume total responsibility for the building. But when they do, the other critical actors would be the architect, the facilities planner, and the state inspector.

Most of the time, the contract for the construction of the building is awarded to a general contractor who subcontracts for all or many of the associated services. The contractor for Cozy Corner, for example, had forty-six subcontracts. Most contractors have a smaller number. The other critical actors are the architect, the facilities planner, and the state inspector.

Sometimes the school district awards the construction contract to a general contractor but, for whatever reason, may hire a construction manager. This person supervises the construction of the building and coordinates the efforts of the architect, the contractor, the state, and the district. The construction manager can be hired without a bid in the state of California. The data for this report indicate that the few school districts who did hire construction managers did not fare any better than those who did not, and in one case, the school built under the construction manager has been a "horrendous experience" for the superintendent and the school district.

These three structures are supposed to maximize the likelihood that the building will be built within the budget and time limitations, will adhere to the architect's design, and will be a smooth process.

The first juncture at which conflict is likely to arise is concerning changes. Changes may be due to the district's wishes, to the state's revisions or oversights, or to misunderstandings between the architect, contractor, or subcontractors. The executive function is to supervise activities and actors, and the professional function is to provide technical and professional supervision. A point of conflict very often is between the architect and the contractor. The executive can provide the distinctions necessary between the two areas of responsibility. The representative function serves to support both the executive's and professionals' efforts.

The second juncture at which conflict may arise is related to adhering to budget and time limitations. Aside from changes causing budget and time extensions, other factors may contribute to difficulties. For example, the contractors may not have interpreted the architect's designs accurately. Contractors sometimes underbid and look for ways to balance their expenditures. The architect and contractor may clash because they hold contrasting expectations regarding each other. The data indicate that it is very important for the architect and contractor to assess each other's capability and ability to work together during the pre-bid conference in order to be able to cooperate with each other and maintain the budget and time limitations during the construction process.

Finally, adherence to the architect's designs is the third area where conflict may arise. The professionals' respect for each other's area leads to better working relationships, which lessens conflicts.

The executive is responsible for coordinating, supervising, and overseeing the total project. The executive's relinquishment of this step to the professionals jeopardizes a smooth process. The professionals—the architect and contractor—exercise their professional judgments within their areas of jurisdiction. The school board and the community provide the support and normative expectations for all parties. It is for this reason that the groundbreaking ceremony assumes both symbolic and practical significance. Responsibility and accountability for all parties are publicly acknowledged. To neglect to acquire this support and commit responsibility and accountability places the project in jeopardy.

It is recommended that the architect-and-contractor structure be the dominant one used in the construction of schools. It is recommended that the essentials for elementary, middle, and high schools be identified and prepared as check lists to be used by the architects, contractors, and building principals during the design, construction, and postoccupancy steps.

Chapter 5

Postconstruction Processes

OCCUPYING THE BUILDING

Interim housing during construction

After the school has been constructed the next step in the process is to open the school. Because the need for schoolhousing has been so great, many school districts have provided interim housing for students while schools are being constructed. A common practice among the school districts in this study was to identify the student body and their teachers and principal who would be housed in the projected new school and provide interim housing for them while the new facility was being prepared. The move to the temporary site was considered as opening the new school and an identity for both the students and school personnel began at this time.

The principal from the Bright Lights Elementary School in the Cozy Corner Unified School District described the sequence of events for their move:

> The Bright Lights students that are there now, started out here. They were at this particular site in September a year ago. In September of this year they moved and I started a new school with these existing buildings. Then next year when I move out another school will move here. Their permanent facility hasn't been built yet so they'll stay here just like we did. One of the nice things is that we already have a school, a PTA, and parent support group in place. I think all of those things will carry over to the new school. I am involved in the process of hiring teachers and support service personnel for the new site. I make the final decision. We receive help from the facilities planner and the business

office person. When we opened this site, there were things we needed, and it was easy for me to get on the phone and call up the business manager and say, "Hey, this is what is going on here." Or call the facilities planner and say, "I need picnic tables and they are not here and school opens tomorrow." They have been very supportive.

In the passage presented above, several activities are identified as part of the move to the new school: the principal is appointed, teachers and staff are assigned, equipment is purchased, students are moved, and parental and community support is developed.

The appointment of the principal

The responsibility for opening the new school is normally the principal's. As stated above, most school districts identify the principal for the new school and provide opportunities for the principal to participate in the construction phases of the school. Sometimes, however, the principal is hired just prior to the opening of the new school. The facilities planner, in most cases, attempts to provide leadership throughout this step. Principals provide professional services when involved early in the process, and during the move they provide administrative services to the new school.

School districts appoint their principals in one of many ways. The principal from Cozy Corner Elementary School in the Cozy Corner Unified School District described the appointment procedure followed in his school district:

I was told in May I would be the principal. I heard about the job through the district's advertisement in the paper. I applied, was interviewed, and selected. There was an individual interview with the panel for about forty-five minutes and as the finalist I had a group interview which lasted for a little over four hours. Some of the interviewers came to my work site and interviewed my principal, the classified staff members, teachers, and students. I also had two written exercises to do before the individual interview with the superintendent.

Most of the time, however, the appointment of the principal comes as a decision from the central office based on some prior evidence that the person may be successful. The principal from Gypsy Elementary School described how she was appointed. Serving as the representative from the Hidden Springs Unified School District, she was heavily involved in the design of the elementary school. Based on that experience she was released from her former position to head a temporary facility located in another part of the district. The temporary building was identified in anticipation of the new school and the children were housed there from September until the end of December. The facilities' materials and equipment were moved to Gypsy during the Christmas break. The children were finally moved to Gypsy in January, but the identification with Gypsy had taken place since September.

During this period, the principal was responsible for hiring all of the staff members for Gypsy Elementary School. Some teachers and students were transferred from other schools. For example, one of the elementary schools sent 250 students and some teachers. Another activity the principal assumed during this interim period was to actively engage more than two hundred parents with Gypsy Elementary School affairs.

Likewise, the principal from one of the elementary schools from the University Unified School District described how his appointment came about.

> I have been the principal here at this elementary school, which is from where most of the Green Wash children will be drawn, and I just assumed that I would be principal over there. This year when we opened both sites, it went very smoothly. The secretaries and I worked long hours prior to school opening. I worked a lot of time over the summer to make sure the opening would be smooth. A lot of parents commented to the superintendent about its smoothness. The superintendent about a month after school opened said to me that I had done a good job starting both schools and that he was comfortable with knowing I was capable of opening up a new school. I did not know for sure, I just assumed all along. After working on the committee for two years, it had become a real important thing to me, become a part of me, and I felt it couldn't be taken away from me. The comments from the superintendent let me know for sure I'll be over there.

The principal from Virginia Elementary School in the Green Valley Unified School District was told in July he would be moving from another elementary school in the district to the new school. The facility was almost completed, but he participated in selecting all of the furniture, supplies, textbooks, and audio visual materials and hiring twelve out of the twenty-one teachers.

The assignment of teachers and staff

The assignment of teachers to the new schools involves districts trying to balance the selection between veteran and first-year teachers. The districts usually want the same teachers to be appointed to both the interim and permanent sites, and most try to coordinate the necessary activities. Districts may choose to hire all new teachers or provide for transfers within the district. The creation of the temporary site provides an opportunity for the principal and teachers to try each other out. The principal explained:

> It would not have been good organization for the board of education and the administration to let everybody from Cozy Corner Middle School to come to Daisy who wanted to because then whoever took over as principal at Cozy Corner would end up with all new inexperienced teachers, possibly a totally new staff. I felt it was wise that the administration left a cohesive group of people that were good leaders, strong at every grade level there and brought over here people of equal strength for every grade level. The superintendent, the board, and the principal made those decisions.

Another principal from the same district explained his participation in this way:

> In order to be ready, I became involved in the process of hiring teachers and support service personnel for the new site. I participated in every panel interview. Probably one of the district-office-level people will be involved. But no one will be hired without my being involved. We make recommendations to the board as to who should be hired. The board makes the final decision.

The purchase of equipment

Principals also engage in readying the building for occupancy. They order, purchase, and move the necessary equipment to the new building before the children move in. One of the principals from Cozy Corner explained this activity in this way:

> In order to get the building ready I work with the director of maintenance and operations. We review all of the specs for furniture and all of the things that are going into the building. Based upon what I need for the program, the three of us decide what to purchase. I deal with purchasing when furniture is involved and with maintenance when I need a stove.

The movement of children

The construction of new schools is usually associated with new-development student groups drawn from the area. The children, likewise, have to be prepared for all of these moves and changes. The principal described how middle school children react.

> The children are excited about the new school. We have tried to keep them enthused. We have to constantly remind them of the safety factor.

And they are very respectful to that. The eighth graders, who I have followed since sixth grade, are sad they have to leave. But they are also excited about going to high school; that kind of takes the crush out of it because eighth graders cannot wait to get out of their middle school.

Gaining parental and community support

Finally, the principal has to insure that parental and community support is gained. Moving to a temporary site requires adjustment from everybody. But most importantly, moving to an interim site delays the socialization process of students, faculty, staff, parents, and community to the new school. Even though the literature (Ernst, 1990) supports a highly organized system of moving to a new school, most school districts have moved according to the need as it arose, and all of the participants have coped accordingly.

Principals attempt to lessen the hardships associated in the moves by providing a stable faculty and staff and by emphasizing the importance of personnel rather than facilities. Sometimes the move is within the same neighborhood. For other schools, the move from the temporary site to the permanent entails moving to a different neighborhood, possibly across town.

Opening a new school for most school districts has involved two steps: moving to an interim site while the construction of the new school is taking place and moving to the new school when it is completed. The associated difficulties have involved developing a school identity. The dedication ceremony is to acknowledge the new school building rather than the move. The principal explains to students and parents how the process will take place and how the district has made provisions for a smooth transition.

The superintendent of Cozy Corner sums up the process simply as, "Well, the Wise Owl Valley School will open in September as a relocatable school. At the same time, construction will begin for the permanent school. Cozy Corner and Eagle Middle Schools will open permanently in September. Usually the principal and I plan the opening of the school."

Moving to the permanent school

Sometimes school districts have no choice but to house their students in buildings that have not been completed. The facilities planner from Green Valley Unified School District related how they had moved the children to Bended Creek School before it was completed:

The construction of Bended Creek was not completed on time, but we had a need to house students. We made sure the classrooms were ready and the office was ready to the point to which it could be occupied. The parking lots were used as the playground. The private sector, the governmental agencies, the contractor, the architect, the fire marshall, and the state inspector working with the school district for the sake of children worked out the plan. The parents were extremely cooperative. We sent them a letter explaining that their children would not be unattended.

Most school districts refrain from moving children to schools before they are completed because their safety may be compromised. Likewise, the construction crew may be inhibited in its work. The usual practice is to have the facilities planner determine the completion and moving dates.

An example of the manner by which the facilities planner exercised leadership during this stage is described in the passage below:

We have a scheduled completion date of November 1st. That is when the contractor expects to be done. We are going to wait until it is ready-turn-key. We do not want to move into the facility when they still have to come to fix something. We want to get everything fixed first. We had some vandalism at another site where a contractor left a door open and some of our things were destroyed. So we do not want to share the site with them. We are covered in the trailers for another couple of months. We planned some leeway. We planned a ceremony for the opening for January. I am hoping that we can get the kids in there in November.

The district's school board approves the opening date for the new school and the children move in. A review of the activities involved shows that in occupying the new school building, a principal is appointed, teachers and staff are assigned, parental and community support is sought, equipment is purchased and placed in the school and, ideally, upon completion of these activities children are moved in. The children cannot be moved in without school board approval.

The appointment of the principal to the new school means that he or she assumes the professional function and administers the activity while the executive provides leadership and the representative provides support. Conflict may arise when the professional function is not enacted properly.

When the principal is appointed late in the process, opening the new school may not be as smooth, due to inexperience or unpreparedness. When the principal has been engaged from the early stages of the construction, the principal may assume a dominant role and supercede the executive. The facilities planner may be unable to exercise the proper leadership role. Normally the principal assumes leadership over the educational personnel and the facilities planner over technical and legal professionals, such as the architects and contractors. Conflict may also arise among the facilities planner, principal, and school board members, parents, or community groups. The representatives may want to play a dominant role in the various ceremonial activities. Fulfillment of the leadership role by the facilities planner is critical during this step.

The dedication of the new school

The formal dedication of a new school facility is important symbolically and practically. The public acknowledgment of the facility assures taxpayers and others that the facility for which they are paying is completed and ready for evaluation. The members of the school site publicly commit themselves to preserving, respecting, and utilizing the building. More importantly, ownership of the building takes place in a public manner.

The principal assumes responsibility for the school's dedication ceremony. The principal from Green Wash Elementary School described how responsibility of the principal is assumed:

> The opening day for the new school ceremony will be my responsibility. There is no official or set format except that something should probably be done. Some organization, a community group, will participate during the opening day ceremony. Local dignitaries will likely be there, along with board members, community representatives, and teachers."

Another principal explained, "Presently, I am on the committee for the dedication ceremony. We have teachers and parents. We will have a few meetings and decide the direction we want to go with an opening ceremony." Another said, "I don't know when the dedication will be. The superintendent will let me know when she would like to have it happen. That's what they did this year when they opened the Bright Lights permanent facility. It will happen in October or November."

The dedication ceremony for the school is fairly traditional. The intent is to acknowledge the completion of the facility, demonstrate that it is working, thank those who participated, and seek the continued support for the institution. The principal of Bright Lights Elementary School in Cozy Corner described his participation in the dedication ceremony of the new school.

We had a dedication in September. When it is a new school they call it a dedication ceremonial. It is kind of dedicated to the district and the community. Usually, the district office and county office people speak. This building was dedicated to the lady who is very much loved and active in the community. We had the state senator, several officials from the county, and people from the State Board of Education. People just give speeches and talk about educational goals and philosophy. But this one was very personal because the lady is alive. When buildings are named or dedicated after a street or a dead person, they do the same type of thing but it does not have the personal touch as when you have someone alive and active as this lady. We did not have a ribbon kind of ceremony. We could have but they did not include that as part of the ceremony.

Most school districts hold the same type of formal dedication ceremonies. The differences between the ceremonies are subtle. The local newspaper reported the dedication of Bright Lights Elementary School in this way:

Hundreds of local parents and teachers, as well as county and state officials honored the President of Cozy Corner Unified School District Board of Trustees, Wednesday night at the dedication of the elementary school. The list of dignitaries who attended the ceremony proved to be a "Who's Who" in education and politics as guest after distinguished guest appeared to honor her. The state senator presented a state flag at the dedication ceremony. The local university's chancellor was among the guests. "It was a beautiful ceremony," said the superintendent of the district. Prior to the dedication, a plaque donated by the school's partner in education, was unveiled. The permanent plaque bears the initials of every staff member at the school as well as the members of the board of education and district administration. The plaque reads, `Together we build tomorrow.' "which I think is a beautiful sentiment," said the superintendent. "It is going to be there forever as a symbol of the school's beginning and that's very special." ([Bright Lights], 1989, C-1, C-5)

Most formal dedication ceremonies are associated with a regularly scheduled school or district meeting. The regular school board, PTA, or school staff meeting is held prior to the dedication. The dedication, too, may symbolize more than the newness of the facility. Sometimes the building is named after an important education person in the area, and the dedication is associated with honoring the person and his or her contributions. Most often, however, the dedication is focused on the new building. The community is informed about the school, the faculty and staff, and the students drawn to it.

Gypsy Elementary School at Hidden Springs Unified School District is an example of a school that held two events associated with the opening of the new school. The principal from Gypsy explained:

> We planned two different things. The first was on the first day of school for our students here. We wanted to have a very brief ceremony for the students, to show them that this is their new school. The dedication ceremony in the spring is going to be a very important formal ceremony open to the public by invitation. We will be inviting dignitaries: the mayor, senators, congressmen, and state department officials. The ceremony will start about 9:30 A.M. The planning process has started. We will have some special things with the students as part of the ceremony. The band will play and the parent community will be involved. The PTA will be assisting us in crowd control and things like that. It is an important day for everyone because it will set the tone for what is going to happen in this school. If we value students and education, and the entire educational process, we need to show other people how we value that. We do that in various ways, by how schooling goes on daily, but also by inviting important officials and dignitaries to show them that we are proud of what we have done; and I think that it is important for our students to see that there is a State Department of Education and they value what we do. We need to provide a big picture for our students and our staff.

The principal of Green Wash Elementary School in the University Unified School District is using the dedication ceremony as the occasion to reclaim the original bell from the first elementary school in the district. Their wish is to incorporate its historical heritage within its dedication ceremony. The principal from that school said, "There are people in the community we would like to invite. East is a very historical location and there is an East historical society that we would like to be represented on our planning committee. We will include someone from the district office. I really do not know what kinds of things we will want to do."

Green Valley Unified School District provides an example of how two dedication ceremonies on the same evening may differ as they reflect the institution's general function and its community's characteristics. Aside from the traditional opening, introduction, and closing rituals, the two schools differed in the emphasis they placed on students, teachers, administrators, and those involved in the construction of the schools. Virginia Elementary School emphasized the administrative ranks and students, while teachers, the architect, and the PTA were noticeably absent. In contrast, the Bended Creek Elementary School ceremony celebrated its students, teachers, and administrators. Neither one acknowledged the architect or contractor, even though the contractor was present at the Virginia Elementary School's ceremony. Virginia Elementary School's student representative explained the significance of its school logo. The Bended Creek Elementary School's principal explained how their opening day was tied to the "Wizard of Oz's 50th Anniversary" time capsule to be buried for twenty-five years and how this will serve to commemorate the occasion every year.

Though both ceremonies had the same purpose, differences in attendance, format, and set-up were noted. One centered around administrative personnel whereas the other centered on children. Neither of the ceremonies referred to the architect or the contractor.

Conclusions

Opening a new school involves a number of activities that are normally assumed by the principal. Cases cited in this study illustrate several practices. Principals may be selected early on, released from prior assignments and later appointed to the new school, or appointed during the latter phases of the new school construction.

The facilities planner exercises leadership in finalizing the relationships between the architect, contractor, and other technical personnel and the educational, state, and local agencies personnel. The facilities planner also ensures that the facility is ready for the children to move in. The representative's function is usually played out by the school board members, parents, and community groups.

Ernst (1990) presented ten steps she believes are necessary for a successful opening of a new school: (1) keep a historical record of the planning, construction, and naming of the new school, (2) establish a strong proactive communication link, (3) select staff, (4) collect placement data of incoming students, (5) order necessary equipment and supplies, (6) provide positive updates, (7) develop relationships with the local businesses, (8) provide preopening social events, (9) make opening day a special event, and (10) provide a dedication ceremony. The data for this study indicate that the historical record is begun early in the process, and the naming of the school takes place by asking the facilities planner and the school board to solicit names from which to select one. Communication and the development of relationships with both local businesses and preopening social events are also activities conducted prior to this step. Opening the school includes the appointment of the principal, the staff, and the assignment of students. After the principal has been appointed, he or she assumes responsibility for the first day of school, selection of staff, purchase of necessary equipment and supplies, the movement of children, and the dedication ceremony.

When the principal is appointed early, the opening of the new school is better coordinated. In the present study, since interim sites are frequently used, the appointment of the principal takes place at that time.

The complications of moving to a new school are greater when students have to move to facilities which are not completed. The most problematic issue is safety. Many school districts do not risk moving children until the facilities are completely ready.

The provision of supplies and equipment and the holding of a dedication ceremony contribute to a smooth transition in the move. First, moving students, faculty, and staff to interim sites and then to the new facility is disruptive even at its best. Avoiding this practice is recommended. However, it is a safer and more secure practice than to move to a facility that is not ready for occupancy. Second, the timely appointment of the principal, faculty and staff minimizes difficulties in the moves. It also ensures that equipment and supplies will be available. Finally, a well-conceived and organized dedication ceremony ensures that the facility is acknowledged and that support and commitment for its preservation and maintenance is acquired. The symbolic and practical significance cannot be underestimated. It is important to link the accountability and the acknowledgement of the architect and contractor for their work during this public event.

POSTOCCUPANCY EVALUATION

Postoccupancy evaluation usually takes place during the first five years of the building's existence. The evaluation begins when the school opens and everyone moves in. The literature, on the other hand, advocates instruments be used to evaluate the school at predetermined periodic times.

Evaluation begins shortly after the building is occupied, when school personnel and the facilities planner receive feedback, complaints, grievances, and compliments. The facilities planner, as the executive, exercises judgment, the professionals provide inspection, and the representative function serves to enforce accountability.

A review of this step begins with a description provided by the school's custodian. Being responsible for the facilities' safety, security, and upkeep, his remarks serve to highlight how school buildings are judged.

The custodian at the Cozy Corner Unified School District described his work in the new elementary school:

> I like this building because it is unique. A lot of adults come in here and they think it is a shopping mall. Just the way it looks when you walk down the hallways because of all the windows on your left and above. It is really an uplifting school. We have a computer room with a lot of Apple GS computers. I think it is a big plus for an elementary school to have a computer room. The library is unique because it is all on wheels. If you notice, all of the book shelves that are in the library are all mobile so we could always change the configuration if and when we want to or get bored with the old set-up type of thing. This building is going to be around forever. It is not easier to work at a new school. The reason is that every dirty mark is going to show. You have nowhere to go but down. You have to at least maintain an even keel because anything that goes wrong, anything that gets dirty, is going to show up immediately. So you have to stay on top of it more so than at old schools. My primary concern is the safety of the staff and the students on the school site. For instance there might be a drainage problem. Let us say, for instance, that it takes some of the dirt, maybe creates a hole or tripping hazard. Or a sprinkler head might be adjusted too high for students to trip over when they are not looking where they are going. We do not want any safety problems here. That is the last thing for a lot of reasons. So I look after safety the most. And then I look after security of the building, making sure that all the doors and windows are locked, and the alarm set on when we are not here. And then, of course, the cleaning. And that takes the rest of my time. I love our new school. I like the windows which are at eye level and the miniaturized furniture. The reception room in the office is sunken so that when the kids come up the counter they can talk to the clerk behind the desk at eye level so that they have a feeling of importance and worth.

The above illustrates the school building's personality and characteristics and how the custodian seeks to enhance and protect it.

The principal's role

Since principals are the ones most involved in establishing their schools, they are the ones who become most aware of any of the building's shortcomings. The principal from Cozy Corner Elementary School said, "Offhand I can't think of anything major that I would do differently than I have done here. Obviously, I learned from this experience of opening a new school. I would probably do a better job of it. It would be more and more of the little things that it takes to do that."

The principal from Gypsy Elementary School in the Hidden Springs Unified School District knows, as do many other principals, that the new facility will not house all of the students, and additional temporary buildings will be part of their physical plant. Gypsy's principal elaborated:

> We are growing very rapidly and we will continue to grow for about another year. We knew that going into the whole process. We planned for that. The school is designed to have a bank of six portable classrooms because according to the state now you must have a certain percentage of relocatables. When we have those relocatables on site, we should be able to house about 900 students. The design took into account the placement of the relocatables.

The principal at one of the elementary schools in the University Unified School District shared his impressions:

> I think Green Wash will be on display as were those other schools the architect took us through. We will end up being a school that other school districts will go through. I look forward to it. The things I like best are the computer lab, multipurpose room, cafeteria and kitchen facilities, and a good library with lots more books. Given the opportunity to be in on the planning and building of another new school, we designed the school to go year-round; less built-in units and close access to storage of rolling cabinets.

The principal from Green Wash Elementary School is dissatisfied with the location of his office. He wanted to be close to the reception area and also the playground. Instead, the teachers, who wanted to be close to the kitchen for easy access to meals, have their classrooms placed in the principal's ideal place for his office. The principal is located directly in front of the school, furthest from the playground, around the corner, and down a hall from the reception area. The disadvantage of this floor plan is that he can enter and leave his office without anyone knowing because he has a door leading to the outside.

Other problems exist: the portables are not placed in a way to enhance the building design nor the landscaping; the parking area for parents is long, stretching along the street, creating congestion for all; and the black top is on one elevation and the field area is on another. Two teachers will have to be on duty to adequately supervise the children. A concession the architect made in his attempt to reduce the dissatisfaction with his modern building design instead of a Mediterranean one was to put a red stripe down the side of the building, claiming this would make it look Spanish.

All of the classrooms have flat roofs and only the office, library, and cafeteria have red tile roofs. The only room-size storage on the entire site is the reference-text storage room. This will be used if they go year-round. All classrooms are "crammed" together and the office is very hard to locate and access. The principal summarizes:

> My overall opinion of the product, so far, is very favorable with the exception of the architecture. I don't like the arches. I wanted it to look mission. I think it's real special. I like the entry; it is a dramatic entry bordered by palm trees. The palm trees on the property add to the landscaping. There are some real drops on our site which makes it interesting.

What is reflected in the case of Green Wash Elementary School is that the building was designed without adequate consultation with the principal. It was assumed the architect and contractor would know how to design an elementary school with its attendant details. The principal has realized its shortcomings upon occupancy.

The principal from Virginia School from the Green Valley Unified School District described the changes he would like:

> One of the things that I find would add to the complex if it were changed would be my office. If it was extended slightly toward the opposite wall and there were two windows there I could see all of the front part of the campus as well as the sides. Then I could monitor the front area completely, including the bus pick-up. Also we need to have in every school—especially elementary—a book storage area. I might even have one more office area.

The principal commented that a new complex provides an opportunity to test everything, while under warranty time, to figure out what is working and what has to be repaired. The most problematic aspect to building evaluation after occupation is that the change will have to be made with children and adults on the premises. The principal said, "Every time something has to be repaired you have to schedule it around the children and events of school. It is not easy because most skilled individuals of the trades hold the same working hours." The associated problem is safety for everybody.

The principal from Virginia Elementary School described the layout of his school:

> There is a lot of space providing for intermingling and ease of traffic patterns. In the building there is a cafeteria/auditorium, which can be opened and serve up to 720 people for a performance. The rear

consists of a gazebo-amphitheater, where another performance can take at the same time. So up to 1500 people at one time can be served. Two theatrical events running at one time in an elementary school is very unique. The capacity of the building is almost 840 students, and portables can be added to max at 1,000. The school is laid out so that the principal has control of the traffic patterns. The kindergarten is self-contained and off to one direction from the core building. Then two A complexes are across from each other adjacent in the back area and the first-grade complex, which is a four complex on the other side. So there is a nice traffic pattern that allows for an openness about the campus. There is also park access.

Another principal from the same school district explained the shortcomings of his school:

You see the urinals were all set too high. They have to tear all those walls out and lower them. That is going to take a while. The whole school is going to be done and the kids aren't going to be able to pee because the urinals are going to be too high. There is also a safety problem. The stage in the back was supposed to have stairs but in the specs a silly ramp was designed instead which the kids will just slide down. Now we have to put all new concrete stairs. So that's why we are kind of fussy on details. The expense is covered depending on where the error came from. The staircase and the urinals are the architect's responsibility. They were his errors.

As can be seen from the previous sections, principals discover that their new facilities have many aspects to be corrected after they occupy the building. These problems may be avoided when principals become involved early in the process.

There are three things the principal from the Green Valley Elementary School District, who moved into the school before it was completed, would do differently if she had the opportunity to open another new school:

Since evaluation of the building began when I moved in, I would be more prepared about construction aspects. I had a lot to learn and often worked ten to twelve hours a day. For example, I had to make a decision regarding which rooms would be controlled by the central computer. Sometimes I had to spend time researching to make a decision on a particular question only to find that the answer or decision had been predetermined by others, or I found that I did not have to make a choice because certain issues were already decided upon by the state, or could not be changed due to state regulations. All the workers I came in contact with were men. They were a bit condescending at first because they did not expect me to be knowledgeable about construction. I came to an agreement with the workers to have input concerning the safety of children and the workers would abide by the state regulations. Also, I established a beautification committee, comprised of parents.

As is evident from the data presented above, facilities planners are not as involved in this step as in the previous ones. Facilities planners, preoccupied with demand, view this phase as "one down, N more to go." The following is a typical remark by facilities planners: "There is no assurance that the new school will not become overcrowded within a few years." Coping with the rapid growth of the community, facilities planners tend to move on to other projects and relinquish the building to principals.

Facilities planners, nevertheless, seek suggestions and advice from teachers and principals who occupy the most recently built schools. These suggestions are then used by him or her and the architects on future buildings.

The superintendent from Distant Place Elementary School District doesn't think that a valid evaluation of the success of a new school is possible after the first year of operation. The superintendent reserves judgment while teachers and others comment and complain. Accountability gets established according to the professionals' and community's satisfaction with the building.

Conclusions

Postoccupancy evaluation is the eighth step in the construction of schools. Most authorities advocate a formal postoccupancy evaluation at the end of the first year and periodic ones for the first five years. The data in this study indicate that postoccupancy evaluation takes place as a series of judgments made on the basis of remarks, grievances, or compliments, starting immediately upon building occupancy. The various functions—executive, professional, and representative—become interchanged as the principal, by virtue of directing the schooling enterprise in the facility, assumes the function of executive by judging the remarks, grievances, or compliments. This reversal of roles is due to the principal's availability and immediate accountability for the quality of the facility.

The facilities planner, on the other hand, is gone from the facility and more likely involved with other facilities at their respective stages. The facilities planner's executive function is very often relinquished to the principal, who assumes both executive and professional functions by judging and inspecting in order to redeem grievances and acknowledge compliments.

This process continues for the first five years, where the principal is the most likely to initiate formal action regarding any correction, change, or claim. The facilities planner enters the process when formal claims have to be lodged and validation from the contractor and architect is required.

The facilities planner also plays a dominant role in identifying design characteristics to incorporate in future buildings. Periodically, facilities planners will duplicate a design. This process is viewed by the facilities planner as exercising judgment in the evaluation of the facility. The representative function provides accountability for the facility at this time. When dissatisfaction for the building is acknowledged, legal and technical action needs to take place. The facilities planner as executive acts to rectify the matter.

As was seen in a previous case, faulty facilities become very problematic for school districts, and support for additional facilities is jeopardized. Postoccupancy evaluation by necessity becomes an ongoing activity until satisfaction, reconciliation with status, and public accountability and verification are stabilized. The principal assumes dominance in this step, contributing to the image and identity of the school.

It is recommended that principals be engaged in the construction of the facility from the early stages and that they participate actively during the construction stage to ensure that their school's design requirements are met. It is recommended that training involving the relevant parties be conducted to familiarize each with the others' areas of responsibility and roles.

A postoccupancy evaluation instrument that accounts for daily judgment and inspection needs to be available.

SCHOOL FACILITY USE

The last step in the construction of new schools requires that school districts consider sharing the new facility with others. Most school districts in this study do not have school facilities available for the use of others; they are instead preoccupied with providing the required facilities for the overwhelming enrollment growth. The idea of sharing their facilities is almost inconceivable. The only indication that school districts share properties with others is when they refer to adjacent park access.

When there is wide participation in the construction of the new facility, the school district and its community's expectations are of intense school use. A norm of protectiveness and possessiveness towards the building is pervasive. When the school facility is built by a small group controlled by the school district, the community and others do not acknowledge its existence. The alienation and distancing from the building means that requests for sharing are not forthcoming and the school district does not extend invitations.

The neglect to consider sharing school facilities does, however, sometimes create problems for school districts. When school facilities are built ahead of residential development, the facility may remain underutilized or empty. When alternative uses of the facility are planned far in advance, the lack of students does not mean a loss for the facility or the school district. This step is directly related to long-range and fiscal planning. When school facilities construction is linked to source of need, and when long-range planning includes contingencies, surplus facilities will be less likely, and sharing of facilities may be a pragmatic option available to school districts.

Chapter 6

The District's Relationship to State Agencies

The steps required in the construction of the new facilities have been presented. The configuration of the executive, professional, and representative functions change with each step. Even though this study is centered in California, most school districts across the nation have to relate to state or local agencies in order to build their schools. The bases for the relationship are likely to be similar. The theoretical assumption is that for each step there is also the requirement that the district relate to the state in one of three ways: regulatory, distributive, or redistributive (Lowi, 1964, 1971, 1979, 1978, 1985a, 1985b.) For the purpose of simplifying the analysis, 'support' and 'fiscal' refer respectively to 'distributive' and 'redistributive'. As was presented in the theoretical framework, *regulatory* refers to a relationship imposing procedures or controlling specifications. The state demands adherence to rules, regulations, procedures, and standards in its approval process. When the state's relationship to the district is in terms of providing funds, the relationship is *redistributive*. Finally, the state may provide symbolic or technical support, referred to as *distributive*.

The next section examines the various types of relationships between the state and school district.

THE OFFICE OF THE STATE ARCHITECT

The relationship between the school district and Office of the State Architect (OSA) is an example of a relationship based on regulation. This office can, but rarely does, provide voluntary preliminary review of the plans and designs, thus avoiding a technical support basis for school district relationships. This review, conducted between the district's architect and the OSA agent, is designed to avoid future problems. When the plans are agreed upon, they are resubmitted for a formal review. This is more surprising when OSA consists of architects belonging to the same professional group of architects as those hired by school districts. The following section describes the process that is followed by the school district in order to comply with OSA to insure facility safety, security, efficiency, and standard quality. The school district will not receive state funding for its facility nor approval for student occupancy without approval from this office.

Plans for new school construction go to OSA at Step 37 of the Lease-Purchase Process and Step 4 as presented in this report. The purpose of this step is to ensure that the structural design and access-compliance features of the proposed facilities are in compliance with the state code of building standards. These include enforcement procedures, fire safety, and material evaluation. In other words, OSA is the regulatory agency that approves the architect's and school district's final plans.

In order to obtain approval for final construction plans, the district architect completes several forms (OSA form SSS-1, application for approval of Plans and Specifications in triplicate) and pays the filing fee. Each check set is made up of a complete set of working drawings, specifications, and structural calculations. If the plans are complete, a number is then issued to the application. No work is performed by OSA until the correct fee has been paid in full, the plans are complete, and (for a modernization project) a letter of certification received from OLA is submitted stating that the cost of the modifications do not exeed 25 percent of the replacement cost of the structure.

Regardless of the funding source, the construction plans are then assigned to structural plan checkers by the plan check supervisor, usually on a first-in/first-out basis. The plan checker checks the plans for compliance with the building code and conformance to the law. Questions that arise during the plan check are referred back to the district architect. Next, the plans are scheduled for the Fire Marshall to review fire and panic safety. The plans are returned to the plan checker, who marks them for correction. When the plan check is complete, the plan check supervisor reviews the checker's work for uniformity and makes sure that all critical points have been checked. The plans are then returned to the district architect for correction.

The district architect must then make the modifications or carefully prepare a rationale for keeping the original design. In these matters it is not necessary for the school district to be involved. However,

OSA does notify the school district whenever there is any interaction with the district architect. Once the district architect has prepared the plans, they are returned to OSA for final approval.

Once the plans are ready for final approval, the district architect, the OSA officials (Fire Marshall, structural safety plan checker, and access compliance plan reviewer) meet at the OSA office to "back check" and to "stamp" the original architectural tracings for identification. This action is done over a period of a day, with representatives present from each of the agencies aforementioned. The OSA plan checker is present. As each page of the plans is turned, all of those agencies must approve it and stamp the original plans appropriately. Upon receipt of a set of the stamped drawings, the application is approved and signed, and a letter of approval is sent to the district and the district architect. OSA does not notify SAB of approval; the architect does.

For an average-size school ($500,000 construction value) of average complexity, it takes about one week to check new construction plans. In addition, about 15 percent of the time the designs are incomplete to the point where additional check sets are needed. These are returned to the district's architect for corrections and modifications. The maximum "bin time" for a set of plans is about four weeks. Bin time measures the time between the receipt of the plans and the time it is assigned to a plan checker.The elapsed time for plan checks vary from one to nine weeks, (including bin time of four weeks). Factors that affect plan check elapsed time include the size of the project, the complexity of the design, and the actual completeness of the design.

OSA works somewhat slower when approving plans that are either of a novel design or call for new or unfamiliar construction materials. For this reason, fewer creative architectural design plans are submitted. Many school districts short on construction time ask their district architects to limit the novelty range in their designs in order to expedite their OSA approval time.

In order for the OSA plan checkers to keep up with new construction products and their structural characteristics, the plan checkers must log time with design and construction seminar classes throughout the year. There are three OSA offices statewide: San Francisco, Los Angeles, and Sacramento. Plan check workload is balanced between the three offices. OSA as a unit within the Department of General Services is supported by service fees through funds paid by school districts. Costs of all work performed is recovered by the fees charged to the districts. The OSA system forces a minimum of quality of design and safety upon the applications from school districts, regardless of the attentiveness by these districts to provide these through the original designs. Further, it acts as a time buffer to control the rate of the state school construction process.

The issues of control and time delay are not viewed favorably by the school districts. The state argues that the delays are really beneficial to the communities because a lengthy review period (1) provides time for the state to determine if the enrollment projections will indeed be realized, (2) minimizes the risk that state policies (such as those concerning handicapped access, structural safety, cost standards, and school location) will be ignored by local school districts, and (3) serves as a rationing device when money is in short supply.

Conflicts of interest arise between OSA, the school district and the architect because the architect's perspective is that the more creative the design, the better. The OSA plan checkers are concerned with safety, expedient review, and high productivity rates, and the architect gets caught between the state agencies and the school district.

The architect interacts the most with OSA, but the school district must maintain a good relationship with all of the agencies. More importantly, however, is that as the architect and OSA review the facility design, compromise regarding the educational program may take place. This is especially true when programatic needs may involve novel designs. The facilities planner must therefore strive for executive control while the architect and OSA interact. Even though the district architects and OSA, members of the same profession, exert influence upon each other, the design and codes process and peer review are meant to guard against preference.

THE DISTRICT'S RELATIONSHIP TO OLA AND SAB

The district's relationship with the Office of Local Assistance (OLA) is regulatory, distributive, and redistributive. OLA provides technical service to school districts and assumes responsibility for regulatory enforcement. The State Allocation Board (SAB) allocates the funds for school housing. The following is a description of the relationship between the two agencies.

The approval process involves specific steps and a variety of forms. The school district's facilities dapartment's support staff work closely with OLA and the state agencies that approve the process. The approval process is lengthy, complicated, and delayed. The time period from initial request to fund construction of a new school to completion of the building averages five years for a high school and two to three years for an elementary school. This process involves many forms that may be wrong, outdated, or badly xeroxed copies sent from OLA to the district to complete. Another difficulty with OLA is the continuity of the process because its high staff turnover rate means different persons for each encounter. One of the facilities planners put it this way:

> In OLA, for example, people come to OLA because their job has been abolished in some other state agency and they are transferred to the OLA where they see what a mess OLA is in and they quit and go someplace else. That has happened to three of my field representatives at the building level. There is no continuity. The present local OLA official, poor guy, couldn't possibly handle all the work he has, he is a good man and he has a construction background, but it's just bureaucracy.

OLA provides guidebooks, handbooks, and responds to districts when they seek assistance. School districts nevertheless complain that everyone in the agencies' system is a bureaucrat. "The system seems to be designed to make sure that school districts are unable to complete school construction quickly," says one of the facilities planners. Some facilities planners believe "it was designed that way because the state knew, going into it, that the state would never have the money to fund it completely. The system is like a gatekeeper to slow down the construction of schools and force needy districts into seeking out alternative methods of fund raising."

One of the facilities planners related that

> They always seem to love forms. I used to go to Sacramento often. Change orders that are four years old have still not had a determination on them. There is always something missing. I was able to get OLA to approve my method of building/designing two schools under one contract. It took me six months to convince OLA, but it saved $800,000 under the state allowable cost. We had to discuss this modification with Sacramento OLA because the local OLA said that they could not do it.

SAB imposes strict guidelines on school districts that request funding for construction of new schools. OLA is the lead agency ensuring adherence to procedure. The facilities planner from Hanging Bridge Unified School District said,

> OLA is very busy and the field representatives are so overloaded that it is difficult for them to be responsive, but they do the best they can under the circumstances. The process is always changing due to the continuous changes occurring in the state approval process. The availability of OLA field representatives is useful for school districts.

The facilities planner for Freeway View Unified School District summarized the source of friction in the relationship with the state agencies:

> I have three new schools under consideration now, each one of these will require an excess of ninety-three different forms, the shortest being three pages and the average about twelve pages. That means roughly a thousand pages of documentation per project. Then you have the State Environmental Input forms and all of the other agency forms. We don't build schools, we just fill out paperwork. The form, 422B, which is the enrollment projection, drives the process of building new schools. It is from that form that you then start filling out the five hundred forms which is a loading-type form.

There is a commonly held belief that the most successful school districts are the ones who are most aware of what is going on (1) in the public realm, (2) in the congressman's office, and (3) in the lobbying organizations who are trying to make school districts' interests into law.

The facilities planner from University Unified School District claimed that in order to maintain positive relationships with the state agencies you have to be sure you coordinate with all agencies. "You know you have been successful in this process when you get the money, when you get the schools built, and when you open the doors."

Some school districts are advised that the field representative for OLA will monitor their progress once they get in line. The facilities planner explained, "There is really very little that a school district must do in terms of the technical aspects of the process. OLA will do most of it. The district need only certify a few forms, combine a few things, and present some data." This activity consists of the school district making lots of trips to Sacramento and tracking applications through the agencies. Often OLA or the other agencies notice a hangup application and notify the district.

The state agencies, OLA and SAB, claim that the school construction process is perceived as easy because the forms are simple but time-consuming. School districts, on the other hand, resent filling out the forms, especially when some of the forms and instructions may not necessarily pertain to their school district. The hard part is accepting the answer. School districts ask for more than they are sometimes eligible for and there is not enough money to do all that the districts want.

The districts' complaints about OLA are summarized in the following statement: "The problem is not that the demand is so great that

OLA could not handle the needs, it is that the present staff is not trained well enough to be able to handle it. Training the staff, setting standards, accountability, and workloads would improve things. These are management problems that can be solved. Streamlining is more appropriate."

After receiving approval from OLA, district allocation is forwarded to SAB. OLA recommends apportionments to SAB. After SAB approves their recommendations, the officials from each agency must meet with the State School Building Finance Committee in order to get the next required approval. Then SAB is able to actually borrow money from the Treasury's pooled money investment fund. The district is notified that its allocation has been granted. Districts believe that they need someone to lobby for them to receive positive agency response. Smaller districts are presumed to be less competent in this regard than the larger ones. The belief is that the allocation of moneys goes to those districts who lobby and maintain legislative contact.

THE DISTRICT'S RELATIONSHIP TO CSDE/SFPD

The California State Department of Education/School Facilities Planning Division (CSDE/SFPD) relates to the school districts on the basis of regulation and support. CSDE/SFPD has been responsible for three areas of oversight: the educational specifications in the design of the facility, the site acquisition, and the approval of the long-range plan. After the Price-Waterhouse Report, the long-range plan was dropped.

CSDE/SFPD plays a major role in providing school districts technical and symbolic support. Most school districts acknowledge this important relationship in positive terms. The next section is a description of these forms of relationships.

Prior to the abolishment of long-range plans, CSDE/SFPD approved a district's five-year plan summarizing the district's status and future five-year projection. The value of the plan was that it forced districts to validate the need for school facilities. Enrollment projections, declines, and other data were compiled to justify new facility construction.

CSDE/SFPD must approve the plans of smaller sized districts regardless of the source of funding. Larger unified districts do not need to go through the CSDE/SFPD plan review. However, with the Lease-Purchase Program, CSDE/SFPD must review all plans in order to certify educational and space adequacy.

Any site that is chosen must be approved by CSDE/SFPD regardless of the source of funding. SAB requires that CSDE/SFPD examine at least three sites per application in order to make sure that the district is getting the most for its money. CSDE/SFPD provides technical assistance to the district. The common practice is for the district to select three possible sites, have the CSDE/SFPD representative come to approve one of them, and proceed from there. The safety hazards or environmental risks are the primary concerns of all the parties involved.

The facilities planner from the Wide Plains Unified School District described the process he follows when he seeks CSDE/SFPD site selection approval:

> The agencies have been helpful in providing guidebooks, handbooks, and answering many questions when my office calls and needs help. The CSDE/SFPD comes and reviews the school sites selected. The persons and offices involved in the site selection for a new school includes the superintendent, facilities planner, and board members. We may pick three sites, bring in the CSDE, and narrow it to two sites. If approved by the SDE, the district narrows it to one final site.

The facilities planner from Hanging Bridge Unified School District summarized his relationship this way: "The CSDE/SFPD's primary function in the new schools process is to grant site approval. As millions of dollars worth of plans are submitted, a rapid approval by the CSDE/SFPD facilitates the total process."

The facilities planner from Hidden Springs Unified School District described the process when complications arise:

> The CSDE/SFPD agent has been down twice to see the proposed sites. One site was in direct alignment with the end of the runway. The second site the developer says will cost two million dollars to grade it. The agent has come to see it and taken the position that he will not approve it unless our board writes officially that we must have it.

As stated above, the bases for the relationship between CSDE/SFPD and the school district are regulatory and supportive. CSDE/SFPD provides general and technical assistance related to the educational specifications in the design of the building and the selection of a site. The relationship tends to fluctuate between regulatory and supportive. The district's request for technical assistance related to site selection and educational specifications, and CSDE/SFPD's willingness to provide it while the regulations and standards are being met, creates a successful relationship that blends both supportive and regulatory bases. School districts, then, have a more positive attitude towards CSDE/SFPD than towards any of the other state agencies.

INTERORGANIZATIONAL RELATIONSHIP

Interorganizationally, school districts are linked to state agencies through regulatory, distributive, and redistributive relationships. OSA is a regulatory agency linking the architect and school district in a vertical interdependency. OSA's rare voluntary technical assistance and OSA's delays in granting approval are viewed by both architects and school districts as an attempt to retain vertical interdependence, especially when this relationship could be softened due to the professional connection between OSA and the school district architects. OLA relates on regulatory and support bases. The agency provides technical support to school districts. More commonly it is the administrative agency of SAB in the acquisition of funds for school building. It regulates the process by which school districts qualify, receive, and expend funds to construct school buildings. The regulatory relationship places the school district in a vertically interdependent situation to OLA. When OLA provides technical assistance, the relationship between it and the school district becomes horizontally interdependent. Most school districts view their relationship to OLA as an unfair vertical interdependent one. The school district's relationship to SAB is vertically interdependent due to the direct fiscal control. School districts avoid interacting with SAB. The school district's relationship to CSDE/SFPD is either regulatory or supportive. Because CSDE/SFPD provides much technical and symbolic support to school districts, they perceive the relationship more akin to horizontal than vertical interdependence. During the course of the study CSDE/SFPD agreed to drop one of its major regulations—long-range planning—which served to reinforce the perception that CSDE/SFPD is friendlier (see Figure 6).

INTERPERSONAL INTERACTION

The state agencies and school districts interact interpersonally in a professional and personal manner. School districts realize that their interorganizational relationship places them at a disadvantage. For this reason, many of the district's officials are reluctant to interact with state agency officials. Most school districts do not deal directly with OSA. The architect is normally given great latitude to conduct all necessary business. The other agencies must, at least on an occasional basis, interact. CSDE/SFPD is the agency that is most accessible and friendly. SAB is the state agency with which most school districts are most vertically interdependent. This section will highlight the personal dimension of the state agencies' and school district's working rela-

FIGURE 6
Interorganizational and Interpersonal Relationships

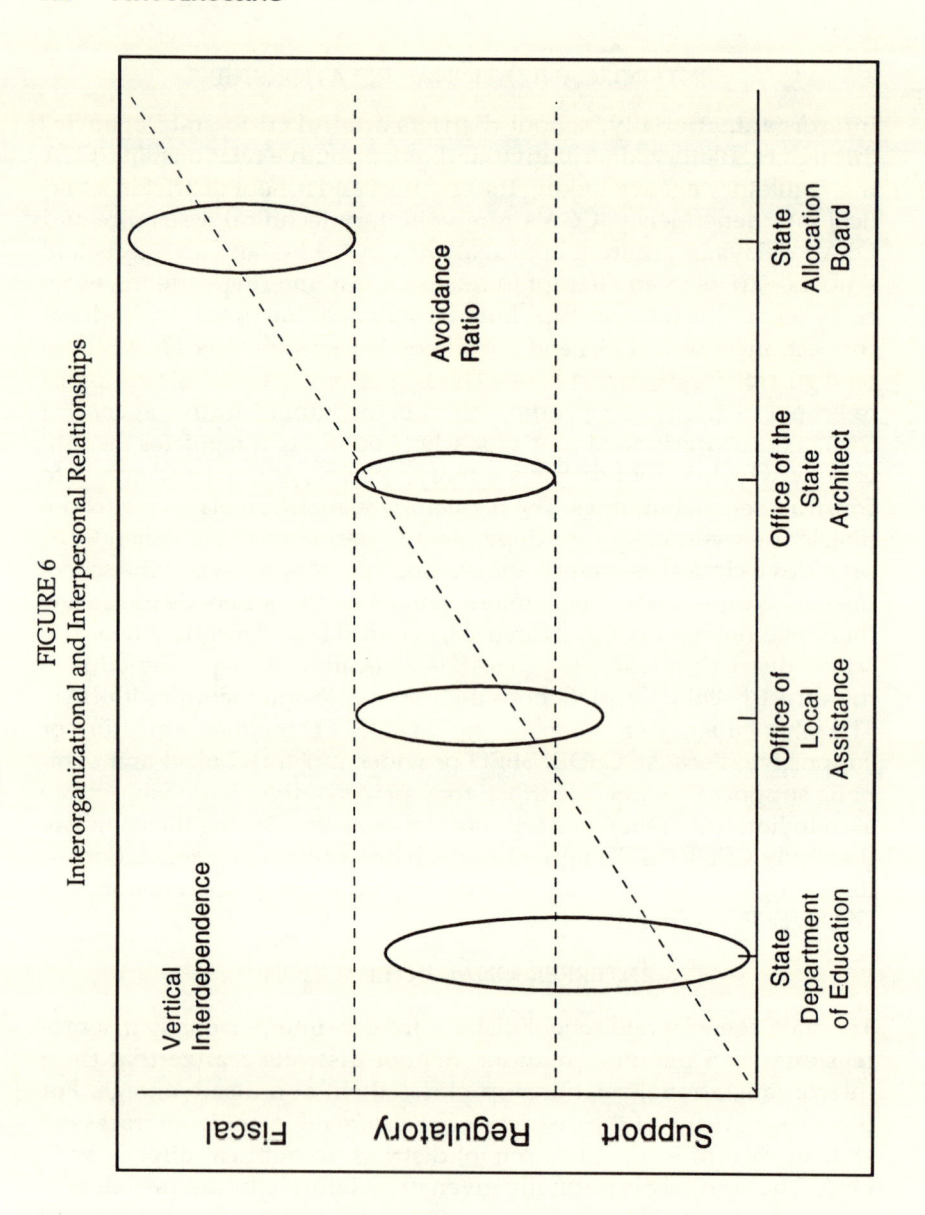

Vertical Interdependence		Avoidance Ratio		
Fiscal	Regulatory		Support	
	State Department of Education	Office of Local Assistance	Office of the State Architect	State Allocation Board

tionship. The facilities planner from Cozy Corner Unified School District described his relationship with the state agencies:

> It is not fair for me to second guess the state. They have a difficult job. They have a lot of audiences that they have to play to and reach. There are one thousand school districts that they have to worry about.

I have always thought, though, that you should keep a system as simple as you possibly can. If you make it complex or structured, you are going to discourage people and organizations from participating. It may be a false feeling on my part, but I feel that if the state could keep the system as simple as possible, things would move faster. I'm sure they would respond that if the system is too simple, you've lost safeguards and control. I think there must be an easier way. I know we don't have the easiest system. Even they will admit that we have a tough system and tough processes.

The facilities planner from Monte Elementary School District explained his relationship to the state agencies in this way:

The forms I have to deal with are very cumbersome. You have to ask a lot of questions because sometimes understanding the various forms is critical and interpretation can be difficult. I have not had many problems to deal with in the processing of forms, but sometimes just getting straight answers is a problem. The process might be expedited if the state field representatives were not handicapped at times from their own departments. At times the regulations and laws and their interpretation are vague and there are gaps in the laws that make the process difficult.

The assistant superintendent from Desert View Unified School District contrasted OSA with CSDE/SFPD:

OSA is a bureaucratic maze that does not need to exist. Architects are certified to certify the buildings to meet with the field act. They should take out insurance policies to cover themselves and do away with the OSA. Architects in general hate dealing with OSA. I think that the OSA architects are the ones who are not capable of getting jobs in a more competitive environment, and thus are less competent. I have handled the entire paperwork process myself. My dealings with the CSDE/SFPD have been with a good person. The official who handles the southern half of the state is stationed in LA and is very accessible and responds within a week. They are very efficient and straightforward. They are only making sure that the location and housing is safe and equitable. Because of the design of the Lease-Purchase process, the interagency fragmentation contributes to tension between the district and the agencies and between the agencies.

As stated previously, one reason the interaction between architects and OSA is workable is because interpersonal relationships between the actors is more likely to be among peers. They are all architects and can relate to each other professionally and as colleagues. For example, the superintendent from Distant Place Elementary School District related to OSA through an architectural firm that served several districts. He has nevertheless gone to Sacramento frequently to visit the various OSA offices.

Some school district's facilities planners claimed that the big problem when dealing with OSA is between the county Fire Marshall and the state Fire Marshall. They have different philosophies and architects are caught in the middle. The local officials say, "I'm going to protect the building and not the kids," and the state says, "No, we're just going to protect the kids." For example, the provision of fire hydrants calls for two from the state Fire Marshall and ten from the city. The state will only pay for two and the city Fire Marshall won't pay for any. Interpersonally, the facilities planner gets caught between the various agencies' officials and the district's architects. In order to sustain their professional and working relationship, the officials relate to each other instrumentally or expressively (Walton, 1972; Evan, 1972). If they relate to each other instrumentally, the bureaucratic characteristics are accentuated. If they choose to relate to each other expressively, their relationship is more personalized. Most facilities planners decide to personalize their relationship with the state agencies' officials. The facilities planner from Cactus Ranch Unified School District explained how this process works:

> I took the people from OLA out to lunch and got to know them. I inquired about their families and related my experiences with theirs. I was the first one finished with emergency portables last year, first one approved and first one finished. OLA, again, for example, will be helpful depending on how you treat them, sympathize with them, take them to lunch, and say, "Hey guys, I need your help." They will help the best they can, but their hands are tied by all the paper work.

The passages presented above show how the school district personalizes its relationship to the state agencies. The state agencies, likewise, personalize their relationship with the facilities planner, the architect, or other school officials.

As stated previously, the facilities planner is the school district's official who most often interacts with the state agencies. However, in the case of OSA, the architect is usually the person who deals most directly with OSA's officials. One of the architects described the interpersonal relationship with OSA:

> OSA is guilty of far too long of a time period in time check. We can draw and design a school in three months from scratch and they will take four to five months to plan check it and that is hard to understand. The state architect says we won't go on it before we bid on it

and we know that the last ten to twelve projects we have done have taken four to five months. That is ridiculous, but we're used to it. So when we tell school districts the real story, we say this is how long it is going to take.

School district officials believe very strongly that the state agencies respond better to a personalized relationship. The facilities planner from University Unified School District explained:

> You have to have a good relationship with your representative. You have to become good personal friends. I came back and took my representative out to lunch and we became good friends. My paperwork is very good. It is difficult for the representative, too. In Sacramento it is just a lot of paperwork, and they keep up with it as best they can as long as there is not too much of a turnover. Some districts have more turnover in representatives and so they experience more problems. I have not had turnovers and have not experienced that. I go to Sacramento a lot too, and I see them when I am up there. I have not had any problems. They are anxious to get through all the paperwork. For example, once OLA needed signatures from the CSDE. I had to get involved because they kept losing the forms. I took the forms, I saw the official and said, "Sign it please." He did and I brought it back to OLA.

The facilities planner from Monte Elementary School District summarized:

> Someone who may have an "in" with someone in Sacramento, who "camps out" in Sacramento when you are processing your documents, makes the system work. As a staff person with the district you do not have the time to sit on the doorsteps of Sacramento and walk these things through. "Massage" the people up there that need to be massaged to get their attention. Otherwise, your forms come in and they sit in an "in" box until somebody gets to them. So you usually retain somebody from the outside to help you through that. Sometimes if you have a full-service architect, they have someone on staff who does that.

CSDE/SFPD no longer issues lists of consultants to advise districts. Instead, school districts are using architects and their own consultants as well as their facilities planners to complete the process. Most school districts eventually realize that it is much more comfortable and effective to discuss questions or problems directly with the state officials rather than OLA. They also realize that an experienced facilities planner will facilitate this process a great deal. Sometimes, however, "A lot of districts take some poor old secretary, make her their facilities manager because the business manager doesn't want to do the work. He sees all those forms and thinks he can give them to her and call her manager and that will do the job," says the facilities planner from Cactus Ranch Unified School District.

The interpersonal relationship with state agencies is between the facilities planner at the school district and an official at the respective agency. Because a vertical interdependence at the organizational level is an uncomfortable one for both parties, individuals representing each organization strive to reduce the tension created. They do this by personalizing the interpersonal relationship. Because regulations, forms, and compliance are such a dominant part of the relationship, top-level executives at the district level and the agency level delegate the responsibilities to their respective staff members. The result of this practice is that in both the school districts and the state agencies, the interpersonal interaction takes place between women. A search for relating expressively or personally with each other rather than instrumentally or bureaucratically resulted in having a large proportion of staff members carrying out paper and interpersonal tasks for the construction of new schools. The implications of this practice is that the executive and professional functions are delegated to staff members, placing the construction of new schools in jeopardy.

CONCLUSIONS

The relationships between the school districts and the state agencies are based on fiscal, regulatory, or support bases. OSA relates to the school district on a regulatory basis, primarily through the architect. OLA relates to the school district through both regulatory and fiscal bases. They regulate the construction process through approval, recommendation of funding, and monitoring the construction process through completion. This lengthy and regulatory relationship places the school district in a vertical interdependent position. Gaining funding approval for school construction increases the interdependency. SAB is the agency that approves and allocates funds to the school districts, creating vertical interdependence between the district and agency. School district officials respond by avoiding interaction.

CSDE/SFPD is the agency that relates to the school district in a regulatory and support basis. Because the degree of technical and symbolic support is equal to or exceeds the regulatory relationship, school districts are more likely to seek interaction with this state agency's officials. The vertical interdependence is lessened if not abolished in many of their dealings.

School districts' officials normally occupying high hierarchical positions resent being placed in a vertical interdependent position in relation to the state agencies' officials. They therefore delegate much of the interaction activity to female staff members. State agency officials respond to this action by likewise assigning their female staff members to interact with the districts' female staff. The consequence is that the school construction business between the state agencies and the school districts is carried on among females. Although the process begins with interaction among males, its conclusion rests with females.

Chapter 7

Conclusions and Policy Implications

The previous chapter has presented a data analysis of the process of school construction and the relationship between the school district and state agencies. The analysis is based on a theoretical framework and draws from data collected from school sites that comprised the CERC membership during the 1989-1991 school years. The process of school construction is comprehensive, lengthy, and consists of many parties and individuals who move in and out of it. This chapter is directed at drawing broad generalizations and proposing policy implications that may be useful to school construction and other projects.

THE THEORETICAL BASIS FOR GENERALIZATION

The analysis presented in the previous chapter is based on cases of school construction in a number of school districts located in the state of California. School construction, as a process, may be likened to any major project an organization undertakes. For school districts, school construction is the most comprehensive, expensive, and complex project it undertakes. As such, it presents an exaggerated case of project activity. Using school construction as a case, the elements necessary for its successful completion are highlighted and become backdrops for analyzing less-complex projects.

The theoretical framework specifies that school construction consists of specified steps that are distinct by virtue of the changes of functions and mix of participants. Even though there is overlap between the steps, each step is distinguishable with a closing activity. For example, the first step (needs assessment) is distinct from the second step (long-range planning) because the executive, professional, and representative functions change. The responsibilities for each of the functions differ in order to carry out the demands of the process. For example, during the first step the executive is responsible for initiating the process of school construction, but that responsibility changes to organization during the second step, which consists of long-range planning. The same thing happens within the professional and representative functions. The responsibility for the professional during the first step is to conduct a demographic analysis, whereas it changes to an advisory role during the second step. Likewise, the representative provides recognition of need during the first step but changes to providing legitimacy and direction during the second step. Any project consists of a deconstructed process, identifying the steps within it, the functions and responsibilities, the parties or individuals attached to each function, and the closing activity.

Most projects require a full-time director for their duration. The data for this report show that school districts do not usually appoint a full-time director or executive to manage the project for its duration. Instead, several persons move in and out, dominating the process, even though the facilities planner is the person most commonly associated with the project. The executive function is, therefore, enacted by more than one person. Sometimes the superintendent initiates the needs assessment step, the business manager assumes responsibilities for the long-range plan and fiscal plan, and then a facilities planner will assume responsibilities during the design, site acquisition, and architect selection step. The remaining steps were also differentially assumed by the facilities planner.

Comprehensive projects run the potential of breakdown at each step. The breakdown is likely to occur because the steps have not been delineated by function and responsibility, the composition of each function has not been determined, or, finally, the critical actors have not been retained throughout the process.

The critical players in the project are the facilities planner, enacting the executive role; the principal and architect, enacting the professional role; and a school board member, enacting the representative role. The logical structure would be one of a task force consisting of those players, with other parties moving and out as necessary. But as has been illustrated by this study, the structure of those engaged in school construction is fluid and ambiguous. When the facilities planner remains active from the beginning to the end, the process by which the building is constructed is more likely to be satisfactory. When the architect participates from the beginning he or she is incorporated into the school district's social system, interacts with the appropriate state agencies, is likely to hire a competent contractor, and is more likely to design a schoolhouse that is more satisfactory to the school personnel and the community. When the principal participates from the beginning, educational specifications are more likely to be met, and the school will be designed with the necessary detail. When the board member participates throughout, the process of school construction is more likely to have support. Other groups and persons move in and out of the process, but the critical actors remain to ensure that the facility that is built is a school.

The second part of the theoretical framework dealing with the school district's relationship to the state agencies is also applicable to relationships with other agencies. Even though the data are limited to school construction processes and relationships with the four state agencies—SAB, OLA, OSA, and CSDE/SFPD—the bases for the relationship to external agencies or other organizations are the same: regulatory, fiscal, or support. Fiscal and regulatory relationships create vertical interdependence. Avoidance between the two organizations increases with vertical interdependence. What is usually conceptualized as communication problems between agencies and persons may be a result of the bases and quality of the relationship. For example, some programatic projects are not successful because the bases for the relationship between the parties are not established.

Interpersonally, the relationship may be instrumental or expressive. By 'instrumental' we mean the use of formalism and neutrality, and by 'expressive' we mean personalized. School districts placed in vertical interdependent relationships to the state agencies choose to interact with the state agencies on a personal basis. This personalized exchange evolved into one between female staff members. A theoretical explanation is that the interpersonal requirements between the district and state agency created identity conflict, which line officials at the school district and state agency avoided by delegating their responsibilities.

GENERALIZATIONS REGARDING ORGANIZATIONAL PROCESSES

The reported case study highlights the coordination of tasks, personnel, and resources. Because the process is so public, visible, and costly, and the product is readily available for evaluation, actors strive for a smooth process. How the executive enacts responsibility for coordinating each of the functions and responsibilities for facilitating the process is very important.

There needs to be further study of communication methods within the schooling process, methods that include regularly scheduled meetings, reports turned in on Friday nights, Monday mornings devoted to review and projections for the upcoming week, and the daily interaction and supervision that take place as the process proceeds. This particular case study shows how the relationship between professionals, technicians, laborers, staff, and other separate offices relate to each other and how the facilities planner retains the executive role in this kind of a mix.

The issue of gender in the mix of this type of a process requires further study. None of the architects or contractors were female.

A project like this requires that the organization and individuals commit time and resources to the life of the project. Personnel turnover always jeopardizes the process to some degree. The second step, requiring long-range planning, is where these considerations are integrated. Many school districts began the project with highly enthusiastic individuals who through time lost their spirit and jeopardized the success of the project.This process is like a relay race in certain respects. For each different step, a different composite of individuals assumes a given area of responsibility that must be fulfilled in a timely fashion to pass responsibility on to the next group at the next step.

When schoolhousing need arises because of development, children await completion of the facility, and while they are waiting, other parts of the organization are being profoundly affected. Overcrowding is normally the most serious effect, impacting the utilization of resources and personnel. A brief period of hardship with a secure anticipation of future housing is endurable, but as difficulties regarding the process become known, the organization's restlessness can turn to hostility and increasing problems. Realistic expectations and trustworthy progress reports delivered throughout the organization and community are necessary to ensure that the energies are expended in support and enthusiasm for the new facility rather than in frustration stemming from inconvenient working conditions.

Organizationally, the distinction between technical and professional dependency and interpersonal trust assumes dominance. Maintaining organizational accord and harmony is an ever-present task for all.

Experience emerged as an important aspect to consider in managing a project. Because constructing schools is an activity that takes place periodically rather than regularly, when dramatic development takes place it is not likely that architects, facilities planners, and contractors are going to be in place with experience and know-how. Inexperienced individuals and firms will necessarily be engaged in the construction of new schools. How do you facilitate the process, given that the participants will be learning their work as they conduct it? One way is to provide permanence to the individuals involved, in order to increase motivation and provide time for individuals to understand their work. The second is in-service training.

The construction of school facilities is not successful unless the building being constructed turns out to be a school. The success is dependent on the permanence of the executive function lodged in the facilities planner, the permanence of the architect, the early participation of the principal, and finally the active involvement of the school board. Those involved in the construction of school facilities must not lose sight of the type of building that is required and needed.

GENERALIZATIONS REGARDING SOCIAL PROCESSES

Because so many groups, individuals, and types of specializations are necessary, the process of school construction is more than a technical task, it is also a social one, requiring a high degree of interaction and a willingness to cooperate, coordinate, and mix patterns of information gathering and transmission. One reason the process breaks down is because at a given step the composition necessary for the conduct is not defined and the parties who are necessary to the step are unable to coordinate their efforts. The person most responsible for ensuring that the interaction takes place, that the relevant parties know each other, and that time is allocated for this activity is the executive. When the executive position is shifted to different persons, this social interaction process may be disrupted and the successful execution of the given step is jeopardized. If there are personnel changes along the way, the process is further complicated.

Another consideration is that this activity is public and the progress is readily visible to outsiders. Parents and the residents of the school building's neighborhood publicly monitor the progress, and interaction with that group becomes necessary. The usual access is through the school district's administration. If the principal has been appointed and is actively involved in the process, the proper conduits for school matters to be transmitted is readily accessible. When the principal has not been appointed, this social activity is likely to turn into a political one involving the school district personnel less closely associated with the facility.

GENERALIZATIONS REGARDING POLITICAL PROCESSES

School district officials work hard to contain the school construction process as a technical task and responsibility. The school board serving as the representative may sometimes relinquish its role and unknowingly agree to contain the process, delegating decision-making to school officials. The data reveal that school officials unknowingly also trigger political responses from the community by engaging in technical tasks, avoiding the symbolic actions, and believing that reduction in interaction will suffice. Symbolic gestures such as groundbreaking, school dedication, and other such ceremonies are proper responses for the school district. The provision of updates are also effective. Newsletters, newspaper articles, written notices, and other media acknowledging task completion or progress reports are all effective. The significance of these activities cannot be underestimated.

POLICY IMPLICATIONS

Several areas require comments regarding the policy implications of this report. The first section will focus on policy implications derived from the issue of school construction, the second section will focus on policy implications lodged in the process, and the third section will focus on policy implications regarding school district and state agency relationships.

School construction policy implications

This study identified the importance of directly linking the source of need for school facilities to funding sources. The three sources of need are replacement of inadequate facilities, population displacement, and new development. The sources for funding appear to be more legitimate and accessible for new development than for either population displacement or replacement of older facilities. This imbalance of attention needs to be corrected. We are at a period where the national as well as the state situation calls for a major school facilities program to replace inadequate schoolhousing, provide schoolhousing for displaced populations, and build facilities for newly developed areas. Replacement does not carry the same urgency as providing schoolhousing for children in newly developed neighborhoods. Cities, communities, and school districts do not have the same sense of responsibility towards displaced populations as they do for newly formed neighborhoods. Newly formed neighborhoods normally consist of parents who can leverage political pressure on school districts and communities to provide school facilities, whereas displaced populations tend to consist of members of minority groups, immigrants, or low-income groups. Their social, political, and economic pressure is slight and can be ignored. The replacement of many school facilities, likewise, may be lodged in changing neighborhoods, and parents or an aging population may not view the provision of school facilities in their interest. Nevertheless, the policy implication is that attention to the three sources of need should be equal.

New development should fund the major portion of school facilities in their areas. Redevelopment and funds from appropriate federal and state revenues should be available for displaced populations, and building replacement should be provided in a systematic way. When the need for new facilities converge in such a manner as in the present, school districts should be able to claim special funds. A policy could be established in which a classification of "disaster" would enable the district to qualify for federal and state funds for the provision of adequate school facilities.

State regulations concerned with facility design need to address the technological advances necessary for the future. The state, to date, has failed to adopt any regulations that encourage or monitor the inclusion of modern technology in school buildings. In the bidding process, procedures and regulations regarding the pre-bid conference should be constructed in order to provide competence to the construction of the facility, but also to ensure that the architect and contractor are compatible and that the facility's design is understood by both parties.

Reevaluating the position of and need for the construction manager (CM) is also advocated by the data collected for this report. At the present time, the CM can be hired without going to bid. One reason it is difficult for school districts to employ CMs is related to the approval process imposed by OSA. OSA deals with architects, and school buildings cannot be built without OSA's ratification. Approval of a design by OSA may be more problematic for a CM than for an architect, so it is necessary for the district to hire an architect to obtain OSA approval. After OSA approval a CM may be hired to apply the architect's design to the construction of the facility. School districts view these necessary steps as complications in the process.

Finally, the issue of the utilization of school facilities is advocated. First, the public ownership of the building needs to be reasserted; and second, empty facilities when the need for new facilities is so urgent appears to be misguided. School districts' long-range plans should include the facilities' use factor to avoid over- or underutilization of school facilities. A system of school facilities community use can be placed under the responsibility of the facilities planner.

Policy implications regarding the process

School construction viewed as project management implies an organizational structure with a permanent executive and meaningful roles for the principal, architect, and the board. The apparent ad hoc structure contributes to a fragmented process and an unsatisfactory relationship with state agencies. One of the most obvious findings in this study is that certain actors appear almost indispensable to the school construction process. It is necessary for one person to act as facilities planner throughout the process. Since the requirement for facilities planners is cyclical, in-service training is as critical as a form of preparatory training. The training and experience necessary for the execution of the position are professional rather than technical. Thus, part of the policy implication is to grant this position executive status. As the data reveal, school districts tended to have the executive function performed by different individuals rather than by one individual. Because the process requires form completion, interaction with state agency officials, many routine tasks, and extensive interaction, this position was many times delegated to female staff members. The dysfunctional consequences related to the differentiated enactment of the role and to the delegation of the executive function to staff personnel have been presented elsewhere.

The inclusion of an architect from the beginning of the process results in a smoother process. The identification and integration of the architect within the school district's social and professional systems ensures that the architect will be more likely to design a school rather than just a building.

Principals familiar with school design details who are brought into the process early contribute more directly to the construction of a schoolhouse. In-service training, however, is necessary to ensure that their interaction with the relevant parties at each of the stages is productive. In sum, it is necessary to have a permanent core of individuals who are engaged throughout the process: the facilities planner, the architect, and the principal. The representative function enacted by a school board member remains active throughout the process and serves to support the process. The function is not expected to require the degree of engagement the other three have, but is expected to be readily accessible at any stage to move in. This is particularly critical during the fiscal planning step. As was seen from the data presented, University Unified School District was unable to pass a general obligation bond (GOB) because it could not justify its district-wide need for an additional high school. Delegation of this responsibility by the school board and the district to local parent groups indicated that the district-wide perception of school need was never fully appreciated. The school board provides such legitimation, and it is the group to mobilize the support needed to overcome special-interest opposition.

Policies regarding funding sources for school facility construction need to be drawn that are straightforward, useful to school districts, and amenable to access. School districts have been provided with a number of funding options, which from the data collected are not readily available to school districts. The five most common sources of funding for school districts are the state, GOBs, Mello-Roos, and developer and redevelopment fees. The other sources are too complicated and require too much obligation for institutions such as school districts. Their officials are unable to benefit from them. A systematic way of obtaining funds for school districts to build the needed school facilities should be developed. The system should provide for the linkage between the source of need and the funding source.

Policy implications regarding school district and state agency relationships

School districts have to relate to state agencies in order to obtain funds, adhere to regulations, and receive technical and symbolic support. The interorganizational relationship is one of vertical interdependence, which is greatest among those agencies controlling funds and least among those agencies performing technical and symbolic support services. The regulatory basis for the interorganizational relationship between the state agencies and the school district increases the vertical interdependence when the legitimacy of the regulation is questioned.

Two aspects of the regulatory basis of relationship merit some examination. First, lodging the regulatory function in OLA and permitting it to provide technical assistance decreased vertical dependence between it and the school district, while lodging the fiscal basis of relationship in SAB increased the dependence on SAB.

The relationship between OSA and the school districts is confined to interaction between the two architects. The characteristic that differentiates the relationship between SAB and OSA, and CSDE/SFPD and OLA, is the provision of technical assistance. SAB could provide fiscal and financial technical assistance and OSA could increase its assistance in school design in order to increase positive interaction between the two parties.

The relationship between the state agencies and the school district is also interpersonal. When actions between the two parties have regulatory and fiscal bases, the two parties strive to avoid each other by delegating authority. The bases, nevertheless, need to be present when projects must be accomplished. School districts might forego regulations and standards, and the safety of children could be compromised. The generalization to be drawn is that there will always be tension between state agencies and school districts because of the inherent vertical interdependence between the two, an interdependence that ensures school districts will respond to social and educational needs.

References

Abramson, P. (1981). The superintendent of buildings and grounds: His job, his status, his pay. *American School and University, 54*(2), 66-71.

——— . (1983). Ninth annual report on educational construction; focus on the "three R's": Repair, refurbish, renovate. *American School and University, 55*(8), 40-42, 44-45.

——— . (1984). 10th annual report on educational construction. *American School and University, 56*(8), 15-19, 24.

——— . (1985). American school and university 11th annual report on educational construction. *American School and University, 57*(8), 23, 25-26, 28-29.

——— . (1986). American school and university 12th annual report on educational construction. *American School and University, 58*(8), 33, 35, 40, 44, 47.

Akers, S. B. (1984). *An evaluation model for secondary school facilities in West Virginia developed in response to the Pauley vs. Bailey decision and the Master Plan for Public Education.* Unpublished doctoral dissertation, Virginia Polytechnic Institute and State University, Blacksburg, Va.

Alexander, L. and Keen, L. H. (1986). *Time for results. The governors' 1991 report on education.* Washington, D.C.: National Governors' Association, Center for Policy Research and Analysis.

Alexander, M. D. and Wood, R. C. (1983). The financing of educational facilities. *Planning and Changing, 14*(4), 201-213.

Allison, J. F. (1988). Relocatable classrooms: An alternative to permanent construction. *School Business Affairs, 54*(1), 24-25.

Ambrosie, F. (1983). Methods for financing school districts. *School Business Affairs, 49*(6), 44, 62-63.

American Association of School Administrators. (1949). *American School Building.* Washington, D.C.: Author.

─────. (1986). *School building architectural directory, 1986.* Arlington, Va.: American Institute of Architects.

─────. (1991). News release survey finds millions of U. S. students attend classes in inadequate school buildings. Arlington, Va.: American Association of School Administrators, 1-3. (November).

American Association of School Administrators, Commission on Open Space Schools. (1971). *Open space schools report.* Washington, D.C.: Author.

Anderson, C. S. (1982). The search for school climate: A review of the research. *Review of Educational Research, 52*(3), 368-420.

Augenblick, J. (1984). School finance in the 1980's, Part I: Alternative approaches to providing state aid for schools. *Spectrum, 2*(2), 38-47.

Ayres, G. (1984). Planning problems and issues with use of educational facilities. *Council of Educational Facility Planners Journal, 22*(6), 15-18.

Barnard, H. (1848) *School architecture or contributions to the improvement of schoolhouses in the United States.* New York: A. S. Barnes & Co.

Bell, C. S., and Coombs, F. S. (1987). Citizens' rating of school district fiscal management. *Planning and Changing: A Journal for School Administrators, 18*(3), 147-53.

Bergman, D. F., and Uerling, D. F. (1985). A functional approach to determine the size of a school site. *Council of Educational Facility Planners Journal, 23*(1), 4-6.

Birch, J. W., and Johnstone, B. K. (1975). *Designing schools and schooling for the handicapped.* Springfield, Ill.: Charles C. Thomas.

Blair, B. (1987) *Long range facilities master plan: 1986-2000, San Diego Unified School District.* San Diego, Calif.: San Diego Unified School District.

Boice, J. R. (1968). *A history and evaluation of the school construction system development project, 1961-1967*. Menlo Park, Calif.: Educational Facilities Laboratories, Inc.

Boles, H. W. (1969). Major considerations in the development of content and method of teaching school plant courses. In *Proceedings of conference on the role of school administrators in the planning, development and management of school facilities*. Athens, University of Georgia, pp. 40-63.

Boughart, F. W. and Trull, A. (1972). *Educational Planning*. New York: Macmillan Publishing Company.

Bowers, J. H. and Burkett, C. W. (1988). Physical environment influences related to student achievement, health, attendance, and behavior. *Council of Educational Facility Planners Journal, 26*(4), 33-34.

Boyer, E. L. (1983). *High school: A report on secondary education in America*. New York: Harper & Row.

[Bright Lights] Namesake Dedicated (1989, September) *The Californian*, pp. C1, C5.

Brubaker, C. W. (1982). *School design—State of the art*. Paper presented at the Annual Meeting of the American Association of School Administrators, New Orleans, La.

———. (1985). *The future outlook for school facilities planning*. Paper presented at the Annual Meeting of the Council of Educational Facility Planners, San Jose, Calif.

———. (1986). Specifications for the design of the school site. *Council of Educational Facility Planners Journal, 24*(1), 14-18.

———. (1988). These 21 trends will shape the future of the school design. *American School Board Journal, 175*(4), 31-33, 66.

Building Systems Information Clearinghouse. (1971). *Building systems planning manual*. Menlo Park, Calif.: Author.

Bulloch, E. W., Jr. (1986). Design and the design process. *Council of Educational Facility Planners Journal, 24*(6), 4-5.

Burlingame, M. (1984). Theory into practice: Educational administration and the cultural perspective. In T. J. Sergiovanni and J. E. Corbally (Eds.), *Leadership and organizational culture* (pp. 295-309). Urbana, Ill.: University of Illinois Press.

Bursch, C. W. (1969). *Forty years of school planning*. Sacramento, Calif.: California State Department of Education.

California Bureau of School Facilities Planning. (1978). *Facilities performance profiles: An instrument to evaluate school facilities*. Sacramento, Calif.: Bureau of Facilities Planning, California State Department of Education.

California Coalition for Fair School Finance. (1984). Local sources of revenue for schools. *School Business Affairs, 50*(2), 30-31, 46.

California State Department of Education. (1986a). *Administration of maintenance and operations in California school districts: A handbook for school administrators and governing boards*. Sacramento, Calif.: Author.

California State Department of Education. (1986b). *Guide for the development of a long-range facilities plan (4th edition)*. Sacramento, Calif.: Author.

California State Department of Education. (1987). *School site selection and approval guide* (draft). Sacramento, Calif.: Author.

California State Department of Finance. (1986c). *An assessment of the need for funding to provide facilities for the unhoused school population anticipated between 1986 and 1991*. Sacramento, Calif.: Author.

Cambron-McCabe, N. H. (1984). The changing school finance scene: Local, state, and federal issues. In T. N. Jones and D. P. Semlar (Eds.), *School Law Update . . . Preventive School Law* (pp. 106-123). Topeka, Kan.: National Organization on Legal Problems of Education.

Camp, W. (1985). Integrate evaluation into the planning process. *Council of Educational Facility Planners Journal, 23*(3), 9-11.

Carnegie Forum on Education and the Economy Task Force on Teaching as a Profession. (1986). *A nation prepared: Teachers for the 21st century: The report of the task force on teaching as a profession*. Washington, D.C.: The Forum.

Carter, M. and Rosenbloom, C. (1989). Compensation survey for school and university administrators. *American School and University, 6*(5), 21-38.

Castaldi, B. (1987). *Educational facilities: Planning, modernization, and management*. Boston: Allyn & Bacon, Inc.

Chan, T. C. (1983). The pros and cons of contractor financed approach to school construction. *Council of Educational Facility Planners Journal, 21*(6), 13.

Chang, V. and Albiani, G. (1987). *Need two-thirds to pass? (No worries). The planning and execution of the Elk Grove Unified School District, California.* Paper presented at the Annual meeting of the California School Boards Association in conjunction with the Association of California School Administrators, San Francisco, CA.

Chick, C. E. (1987). Last in; First out maintenance budgets. *Council of Educational Facility Planners Journal, 25*(4), 4-6.

Cleland, W. B. (1984). The cost of design services: Problems and issues from the owner's view. *Council of Educational Facility Planners Journal, 22*(6), 7-9.

Cold, B. (1986). *Architecture as a quality in the learning and teaching process.* Paper presented at the Edusystems 2000 International Congress on Educational Facilities, Values, and Contents, Jerusalem, Israel.

Coley, J. D. (1988). A practitioner's perspective on school facilities. *School Business Affairs, 54*(8), 20-24.

Commission on California State Government Organization and Economy. (1978). *A study of the utilization of public school facilities, grades K-12.* Sacramento, Calif.: Author.

Council of Educational Facility Planners. (1969). *Facility technology: Catalyst for learning.* Columbus, Ohio: Author.

Council of Educational Facility Planners, International. (1980). *Energy Use in Community Schools.* Columbus, Ohio: Author.

———. (1985). *Guide for planning educational facilities: An authoritative and comprehensive guide to planning of educational facilities from the conception of need through utilization of the facility.* Columbus, Ohio: Author.

———. (1986a). *Space planning guidelines.* Columbus, Ohio: Author.

———. (1986b). *Guide for planning educational facilities.* Columbus, Ohio: Author.

Davis, C. and Steentofte, K. (1988). *School facilities institute: A basic course manual.* Sacramento, Calif.: California State Department of Education.

Davis, J. and Loveless, E. E. (1981). *The administrator and educational facilities*. New York: University Press of America.

Day, C. W. (1983a). The shape of schools to come. *American School and University, 56*(3), 7-8.

―――. (1983b). Avoiding conflicts in facility planning. *School Business Affairs, 49*(5), 24.

―――. (1984). Determining school capacity. *School Business Affairs, 50*(7), 14-15.

―――. (1985a). Architect-school client conflicts: Project construction. *School Business Affairs, 51*(8), 26.

―――. (1985b). Architect-school client conflicts: The contractual agreement. *School Business Affairs. 51*(7), 25.

―――. (1985c). Conflicts: Owners v. architects. *Council of Educational Facility Planners Journal. 23*(6), 4-5.

―――. (1985d). Who affects costs of constructing school facilities? *Council of Educational Facility Planners Journal, 23*(6), 9-10.

Day, C. W. and Groten, J. P. (1986). How well do you know school construction? *School Business Affairs, 52*(11), 44-47.

Day, C. W. and Speicher, A. D. (1985). *State of the art facility: A planning process*. Paper presented at the Annual Meeting of the Association of School Business Officials, Las Vegas, Nev.

Delany, J. B. (1983). School construction scheduling. *Council of Educational Facility Planners Journal, 21*(5), 8-9.

Department of Finance, Program Evaluation Unit. (1980). *A study on school facilities utilization and maintenance*. Sacramento, Calif.: Author.

Dressler, F. B. (1911). *American schoolhouses*. Washington, D. C.: United States Government Printing Office.

Drexel, Burnham & Lambert, Inc. (1989). *The Mello-Roos community facilities act handbook: A guide to issues and developers*. Beverly Hills, Calif.: Author.

Duke, D. L. and Perry, C. (1978). Can alternative schools succeed where Benjamin Spock, Spiro Agnew and B. F. Skinner have failed? *Adolescence, 13*, 375-92.

Dugmore, A. R. (1903). New citizens for the republic. *The World's Work,* 5(6), 3323-26.

Dunham, A. G. and Marmar, T. R. (1978). Federal policy and health: Recent trends and differing perspectives. In T. J. Lowi and A. Stone (Eds.) *Nationalizing government: Public policies in America* (pp. 263-98). Beverly Hills, Calif.: Sage.

Earthman, G. I. (1984). Problems and alternatives in housing students: What a school business administrator should know. *Journal of Education Finance,* 10(2), 150-71.

————. (1985a). Evaluating the completed project. *Council of Educational Facility Planners Journal,* 23(3), 5-6.

————. (1985b). Evaluating the impact of the building environment on the individual. *Council of Educational Facility Planners Journal,* 23(4), 15-17.

————. (1986). *Facility planning and management: Principles of school business management.* Reston, Va.: Association of School Business Officials International.

————. (1987). A window on the future at the annual meeting: Experts' reactions. Annual International Conference of the Council of Educational Facility Planners, International. *Council of Educational Facility Planner Journal,* 25(2), 18-20.

Educational Facilities Laboratories, Inc. (1960). *The Cost of a Schoolhouse.* New York: Author.

————. (1967). *SCSD: The project and the schools.* New York: Author.

Education Writers Association (1989). *Wolves at the schoolhouse door: An investigation of the condition of public school buildings.* Washington, D.C.: Author.

Eismann, D. (1976). *Schools and neighborhood research study: School building use study.* Washington, D.C.: National Institute of Education.

Elhanini, A. (1986). *Educators, architects and the Tower of Babel.* Paper presented at the Edusystems 2000 International Congress on Educational Facilities, Values, and Contents, Jerusalem, Israel.

Elmore, R. F. (1979-80). Backward mapping: Implementation research and policy decisions. *Political Science Quarterly,* 94(4), 608.

Engelhardt, N. L. (1970). *Complete guide for planning new schools*. West Nyack, N.Y.: Parker Publishing Co.

English, F. W. (1992). *Educational administration: The human side*. New York: Harper Collins.

Ernst, C. P. (1990). Planning and management: Opening a new school. *Thrust, 20*, 4-45.

Epperson, D. R. (1983). Construction contract changes. *Council of Edculational Facility Planners Journal, 21*(5), 6-8.

Evan, W. M. (1972). An organization-set model of inter-organizational relations. In M. Tuite, R. Chisom and M. Radnor (Eds.), *Inter-organizational decision making* (pp. 181-200). Chicago: Aldine Publishing Co.

Eveleth, S. J. (1870). *School-house architecture*. New York: The American News Co.

Everett, R. E. (1986). Educational specifications for administrative and support areas in school buildings: Considerations in planning. *Council of Educational Facility Planners Journal, 24*(1), 25-27.

Ficklen, E. (1983). This school's unusual design solves an architectural puzzle beautifully. *American School Board Journal, 170*(7), 34.

Flagg, J. T. (1964). *The organizational climate of schools: Its relationship to pupil achievement, size of school, and teacher turnover*. Unpublished doctoral dissertation, Rutgers University, New Brunwick, N.J.

Frederick, G. W, Galvin, K. M. and Book, C. L. (1976). *Growing together— Classroom communication*. Columbus, Ohio: Charles E. Merrill.

French, W. C. (1965). *The high school principal and staff in the crowded school*. New York: Teachers College.

Gallup, A. (1985). *Phi Delta Kappa gallup poll of teachers' attitudes toward the public schools*. Bloomington, Ind.: Phi Delta Kappa.

Gibbons, N. L. (1985). Secondary school capacity, room needs or utilization. *Council of Educational Facility Planners Journal, 23*(3), 12-14.

Gipson, J. (1985). *Annotated bibliography on school finance: Policy and political issues; federal government; state issues; non-public schools; accountability*. Detroit: Department of Administrative and Organizational Studies, Wayne State University.

Glass, T. E. (1986). Educational specifications: A blueprint for the future program. *Council of Educational Facility Planners Journal, 24*(1), 4-13.

Goldberg, W. H. (1983). *Mergers, motives, modes, methods.* England: Gower Publishing Co.

Goldblatt, S. M. and Wood, R. C. (1983). Financing educational facility constructions: Prevailing wage litigation. In T. N. Jones and D. P. Selmer (Eds.), *School Law Update* (pp. 269-93). Topeka, Kan.: National Organization in Legal Problems of Education.

——— . (1985). Construction management for educational facilities: Professional services' procurement and competitive bid statutes. In T. N. Jones and D. P. Selmer (Eds), *School Law Update 1985* (pp. 18). Topeka Kan.: National Organization on Legal Problems of Education.

Goodlad, J. I. (1984). *A place called school: Prospects for the future.* New York: McGraw-Hill Book Co.

Graves, B. E. (1983). Guide to alternatives for financing school buildings. *Council of Educational Facility Planners Journal, 21*(6), 7.

——— . (1984a). Assessing facility needs and developing a management program. *Council of Educational Facility Planners Journal, 22*(5), 4-9.

——— . (1984b). Facility planning. *American School and University, 56*(6), 20.

Gross, R. and Murphy, J. (1968). *Educational change and architectural consequences: A report on facilities for individualized instruction.* New York: Educational Facilities Laboratories.

Groves, R. (1985). The architect and school administrator relationship during construction of school facilities: Contract administration. *Council of Educational Facility Planners Journal, 23*(2), 4-6.

Gump, P. V. (1980). The school as a social situation. *Annual Review of Psychology, 31*, 553-82.

Hansen, K. H. (1979). *State educational policy and the Proposition 13 movement, An overview of policy issues.* Portland, Ore.: Northwest Center for State Educational Policy Studies.

Hansen, S. J. (1985). This time, let's put energy conservation on the blueprint for new schools. *American School Board Journal, 172*(6), 38-39.

Hansen, S. J. Associates, Inc. (1984). *School finance and energy through the year 2000*, Lake Jackson, Tex.: Author.

Hargraves, D. and Vanwechel, P. (1987). How to maintain project control via checkpoint. *School Administrator, 44*(6), 17-20.

Haun, G. and Earthman, G. (1983). Alternative contractual relationships for construction of facilities. *Council of Educational Facility Planners Journal, 21*(5), 10-12.

Hawkins. H. L. (1977). *Appraisal guide for school facilities*. Midland, Mich.: Pendell Publishing Co.

─────. (1985). Physical space: From concept to reality. *Council of Educational Facility Planners Journal, 23*(4), 11-14.

─────. (1986). School facilities: A component of educational reform? *Council of Educational Facility Planners Journal, 24*(6), 23-25.

Hawkins, H. L. and Lilley, H. E. (1986). *Guide for school facility appraisal, 1986 edition*. Columbus, Ohio: Council of Educational Facility Planners, International.

Hawkins, H. L. and Overbaugh, B. L. (1988). The interface between facilities and learning. *Council of Educational Facility Planners Journal, 26*(4), 4-7.

Hedley, R. L. and Brokaw, J. C. (1984). Facility planner and architect as the planning and design team: Problems and issues. *Council of Educational Facility Planners Journal, 22*(6), 4-7.

Herron, P. L. (1983). The contractor as a participant in financing capital construction. *Council of Educational Facility Planners Journal, 21*(6), 11-13.

Hertz, K. V. and Day, C. W. (Eds.). (1987). *Schoolhouse planning*. Reston, Va.: Association of School Business Officials International.

Heydt, H. J. (1988). School housing in California: A multi-billion dollar business facing a severe funding crisis. *The Council of Educational Facility Planners International, 26*(3), 11-13.

─────. (1991). *School Facilities Planning Division fingertip facts about school facilities*. Sacramento, Calif.: School Facilities Planning Division, State of California.

Hill, F. (1983). The need for coordination between educational facility planning and urban land use planning: A case study. *Council of Educational Facility Planners Journal, 21*(3), 4-6.

———. (1986). *Facility planning for the 21st century: Technology, industry, and education.* Paper presented at the Edusystems 2000 International Congress on Educational Facilities, Values, and Contents, Jerusalem, Israel.

———. (1987). How to plan tomorrow's schools today. *School Administrator, 44*(6), 10-12.

Hill, J. C. (1984). Performance-based evaluation of school facilities, *Council of Educational Facility Planners Journal, 22*(2), pp. 8-12.

Holt, S. L. (1987). State education agency services: Limitations and prerequisites for change. *Planning and Changing, 18*(3), 170-77.

Hudson, C. (1988). Financing public elementary and secondary school facilities in Nebraska, *Journal of Education Finance, 31*(3), 338-41.

Hultgren, S. (1985). Why schools choose construction managers. *Council of Educational Facility Planners Journal, 23*(6), 7-9.

Insel, P. M. and Moos, R. H. (1974). Psychological environments: Expanding the scope of human ecology. *American Psychologist, 29,* 179-88.

Jenkins, J. (Ed.) (1985). *Guide for planning educational facilities. An authoritative and comprehensive guide to the planning of educational facilities from the conception of need through the utilization of the facility. Eighth edition.* Columbus, Ohio: Council of Educational Facility Planners, International.

Jenkins, J. (1986). Dwayne E. Gardner: A professional profile. *Council of Educational Facility Planners Journal, 24*(2), 4-8.

Jilk, B. A. (1987). Boomers' kids pose new school construction questions. *School Administrators, 44*(6), 14-15.

Jordan, K. (1988). Financing capital outlay and debt service in Arizona. *Journal of School Finance, 13*(3), 290-96.

Karst, R. R. (1984). A composium of school facility quality with teachers and pupil user attitudes. *Council of Educational Facility Planners Journal, 22*(4), 21-22.

Kaufman, H. (1956). Emerging conflicts in the doctrine of public administration. *American Political Science Review, 50*(4), 1057-73.

Keck, D. B. (1978). *The development of a model for the post-occupancy evaluation design of educational facilities.* Doctoral dissertation, Ohio State University, Columbus, Ohio.

Keough, K. E. and Earthman, G. I. (1984). Questions facility planners should ask about the future. *Council of Educational Facility Planners Journal, 22*(6), 13-15.

King, D. & Kimbrough, T. (1982). *Financing the school plant.* Paper presented at the Annual Meeting of the Council of Educational Facility Planners, International. Columbus, Ohio.

Kirschenstein, J. (1980). Planning for the public schools: Infrastructure fee and developer responsibilities. *Council of Educational Facility Planners Journal, 18*(1), 4-5.

Kluenker, C. (1986). Construction management: Exploding some myths. *Council of Educational Facility Planners Journal, 24*(2), 13-15.

Knirk, F. G. (1979). *Designing productive learning environments.* Englewood Cliffs, N.J.: Educational Technology Publications.

Kowalski, T. J. (1989). *Planning and Managing School Facilities.* New York: Praeger.

Kutkat, J. H. (1983). Keep the lid on school construction costs through precise planning. *American School Board Journal, 170*(7), 30-31.

Landes, J. L. and Sumption, M. K. (1957). *Citizens workbook for evaluating school buildings.* New York: Harper & Row.

Leu, D. J. (1965). *Planning educational facilities.* New York: Center for Applied Research in Education.

Lewis, M. (1990, December). Maternity wards delivering bad news to state officials. *The Press—Enterprise,* p. A-3.

Lezotte, L. W. and Passalcqua. J. (1978). Individual school buildings: Accounting for differences in measured pupil performance. *Urban Education, 13,* 283-93.

L'Hote, J. D. (1983). Educational facility construction: A role for the owner. *Council of Educational Facility Planners Journal, 21*(5), 4-6.

Lindley, C. (1985). Enhancement through landscaping, *Council of Educational Facility Planners Journal,* 23 (4), 4-7.

Lloyds Laboratories, Inc. and D. G. King Assoc. (1987). "Demographics for California School Construction Funding, 'Simplifed.'" Alta Loma, Calif.

———. (1987). "Overview of California School Construction Funding Simplified." Alta Loma, Calif.

Lowi, T. J. (1964). *At the pleasure of the Mayor.* London: The Free Press of Glencoe.

———. (1971). *The politics of disorder.* New York: Basic Books.

———. (1979). 2nd ed. *The end of liberalism.* New York: W. W. Norton & Co.

———. (1985a). *The personal president: Power invested, promise unfulfilled.* Ithaca, N.Y.: Cornell University Press.

———. (1985b). Why is there no socialism in the United States? *Society,* 22(2), 34-42.

Lowi, T. J. and Stone, A. (Eds.). (1978). *Nationalizing government: Public policies in America.* Beverly Hills, Calif.: Sage.

Lows, R. L. (1987). Enrollment projection: A methodology for eras of growth and decline. *Council of Educational Facility Planners Journal,* 25(3), 4-7.

Lutz, F. W., Betz, L. E., and Maddirola, J. S. (1987). *The Texas School Facilities Study: 1986-1996.* Commerce, Texas: East Texas State University.

MacConnell, J. D. (1957). *Planning for school buildings.* Englewood Cliffs, N.J.: Prentice Hall, Inc.

MacConnell, J. D. and Associates, Inc. (1989). *First phase of a long-range facilities interactive and development plan.* Palo Alto, Calif.: Authors.

MacKenzie, D. G. (1989). *Planning Educational Facilities.* New York: University Press of America.

Maintenance Gap: Deferred Repair and Renovation in the Nation's Elementary and Secondary Schools. A Joint Report. (1981). Arlington, Va.: American Association of School Administrators.

Manning, P. (1967). *The primary school: An environment for education.* Liverpool, England: Rockliff Bros., Limited.

Mayfield, J. (1984). *Towards responsive building policies.* Paris, France: Organization for Economic Cooperation and Development.

McClintock, J. and McClintock, R. (Eds.). (1970). *Henry Barnard's school architecture.* New York: Teachers College Press.

McGuffey, C. W. (1974). *MEEB: Model for the evaluation of educational buildings.* Prepared for Simi School, Chicago Board of Education. Unpublished manuscript.

———. (1982). Facilities. In H. J. Walbey (Ed.), *Improving educational standards and productivity: The research basis for policy* (pp. 237-88). Berkeley, Calif.: McCutchen Pub. Co.

McGuffey, C. W. and Argo, R. (1984). The electronic spreadsheet: A facilities planning tool. *Council of Educational Facility Planners Journal,* 22(5), 23-26.

McGuire, C. K. (1983). *School facilities and deferred maintenance. Issuegram 43.* Denver: Education Commission of the States.

McQuade, W. (Ed.) (1958). *Schoolhouse.* New York: Simon & Schuster.

Mills, E. D. (Ed.). (1976). *Planning: Buildings for education, culture and science.* Huntington, N.Y.: Krieger.

Minzey, J. D. and Townsend, A. C. (1984). *Core plus education. A model for schools of the future.* Flint, Mich.: Mott Foundation.

Miskel, C. and Ogawa, R. (1988). Work motivation, job satisfaction and climate. In N. Boyen (Ed.), *Handbook of research on educational administration* (pp. 279-304). New York: Longman.

Moos, R. H. (1976). *The human conflict: Environmental determinants of behavior.* New York: Wiley.

Morocco, J. C. (1978). The relationship between the size of elementary schools and pupil perception of their environment. *Education.* 98, 451-54.

New York State Department of Education, Bureau of School Program Evaluation. (1976). *Which school factors relate to learning? Summary of findings of three sets of students.* Albany, N.Y.: New York State Department of Education.

Nisbet, J., Hendry, L., Steward, C., and Watt, J., with the assistance of Ann Byatt. (1980). *Towards community education*. Great Britain: Aberdeen University Press.

Odden, A. (1986). *School finances, reform, and revenue needs*. School of Education and Policy Analysis for California Education; Stanford, Calif.: Stanford University School of Education.

Organization for Economic Cooperation and Development. (1978). *Building for school and community: Policies and strategies*. France: Author.

Ornstein, A. C. (1988). State financing of public schools: Policies and prospects. *Urban Education, 23,* 188-207.

Palmer, A. M. (Ed.). (1975). *Research centers directory. Fifth edition.* Detroit, Mich.: Gale Research Company Book Tower.

Pauley v. Bailey, Circuit Court of Kanawha County, West Virginia, no. 75, 1268, May 11, 1982, p. 165.

Pauley v. Bailey no. 16232. Supreme Court of Appeals of West Virginia, December 12, 1984. *324 South Eastern Reporter, 2nd Series,* West Virginia, 128-38.

Pennings, J. (1978). *Interlocking directorates: A selective review and proposal,* Working paper No. 20-77-78. Pittsburgh, Pa.: Carnegie-Mellon University.

———. (1981). Strategically interdependent organizations. In P. C. Nystrom and W. H. Starbuck (Eds.) *Handbook of organizational design, Volume I.* New York: Oxford University Press.

Pennings, J. and Goodman, P. S. (1977). Towards a workable framework. In P. S. Goodman and J. Pennings (Eds.), *New perspective of organizational effectiveness.* San Francisco: Jossey Bass.

Phi Delta Kappa. (1980). Financing facilities. *American School and University, 61*(9), 50-51.

Pierce, R. A. (1989). Financing facilities. *American School and University, 61*(9), 50, 52.

Plumley, J. P. (1978). *The impact of school building age on the academic achievement of pupils from selected schools in the state of Georgia.* Unpublished doctoral dissertation. Athens, Ga.: University of Georgia.

Price-Waterhouse. (1988). *Final report, school facilities management*. Sacramento, Calif.: Author.

Reida, G. W. (1962). *A manual for evaluating school facilities*. Topeka, Kan.: State Department of Public Instruction.

Roth, A. (1966). *The new schoolhouse. 4th Revised edition*. New York: Frederick A. Praeger.

Rutter, M. Moreghan, B., Mortimore, P., and Ouston, J. (1979). *Fifteen thousand hours: Secondary schools and their effect on children*. Cambridge, Mass.: Harvard University Press.

Samption, M. R. and Landes, J. W. (1957). *Planning functional school building*. New York: Harper & Row.

School Facilities and Transportation Division, California State Department of Education (1986). *Guide for the development of a long-range facilities plan*. Sacramento, Calif.: Author.

Seaborne, M.V.J. (1971). *Primary school design*. London: Routledge & Kegan Paul.

Seattle Public Schools, Washington, University, and Seattle Bureau of Schools. (1976). *Schools and neighborhoods research study: Neighborhood impact study, final report*. Washington, D. C.: National Institute of Education.

Sendor, B. B. (1985). Financing school construction: A primer. *School Law Bulletin, 16*(1), 1-8.

Serrano v. Priest. (1974). 18 Cal. 3d. 728; 135 Cal. Rptr. 345. Affirmed, 12-30-76.

Sinclair, R. L. (1970). Elementary school educationl environment: Toward schools that are responsive to students. *National Elementary Principal, 49*(5), 53-58.

Sizer, T. R. (1984). *Horace's compromise: The dilemma of the American high school*. Boston: Houghton Mifflin.

Smit, D. and Hesse-Wallace, R. (Eds.). (1980). *Alternatives for financing school construction in Eugene Public School District 4J*. Eugene, Oregon: Eugene School District, Oregon.

Smith, E. (1984). Follow these nine steps to select the architectural firm that can design a new school according to your exact specification. *American School Board Journal, 171*(5), 36-37.

Smith, L. M., Dwyer, D. C., Pruty, J. J., and Kleine, P. F. (1988). *Innovation and change in schooling: History, politics and agency.* London: The Falmer Press.

Smith, L. M. and Keith, P. M. (1971). *Anatomy of educational innovation: An organizational analysis of an elementary school.* New York: John Wiley & Sons.

Smith, P. B. (1986). How much is enough? Insurance requirements in construction contracts. *Council of Educational Facility Planners Journal, 24*(6), 6-8.

South Carolina State Department of Education, Office of School Planning and Building. (1983). *South Carolina school facilities planning and construction guide.* Columbus, S.C.: Author.

State Allocation Board. (1989). *Report of the executive officer: Current status of the Price-Waterhouse report.* Sacramento, Calif.: Author.

Stewart, G. K. (1985). Some old questions revisited. *Council of Educational Facility Planners Journal, 23*(5), 12-14.

Strayer, G. D. and Engelhardt, N. L. (1923). *Standards for elementary school building.* New York: Columbia Teachers College.

Strevell, W. H. and Burke, A. J. (1959). *Administration of the school building program.* New York: McGraw-Hill.

Swenson, E. S. (1987). Climbing Mt. Technology with smart buildings. *Council of Educational Facility Planners Journal, 25*(2), 21-23.

Sylvester, T. S. (1988). Relocatable and modular classrooms: Booming business. *School Business Affairs, 54*(1), 22-23.

Taguiri, R. (1968). The concept of organizational climate. In R. Taguiri and G. H. Litevin (Eds.), *Organizational climate: Explanation of a concept.* Boston: Harvard University.

Tanner, C. K. (1985). Planning and site selection involving groups. *Council of Educational Facility Planners Journal, 23*(2), 10-12.

Thompson, D. (1988). Providing for capital improvement projects in Hawaii. *Journal of Education Finance, 13*(3), 24-27.

Truby, R. (1983). Pauley v. Bailey and the West Virginia Master Plan. *Phi Delta Kappan, 65*(4), 284-86.

Tucker, M. and Mandel, D. (1986). The Carnegie report—A call for redesigning the schools. *Phi Delta Kappan, 68*(1) pp. 24-27.

United Nations Educational, Scientific, and Cultural Organization. (1981). *Educational facilities thesaurus.* Paris, France: Division of Educational Policy and Planning.

USA Weekend, "If Teens had money, they'd buy decent buildings," August 23-25, 1991 (p.8). New York: Gannet Co., Inc. *USA Weekend.*

Walton, R. E. (1972). Interorganizational decision making and identity conflict. In M. Tuite, R. Chisolm, and M. Radnor (Eds.), *Interorganizational decision making.* Chicago: Aldine Publishing Co.

Weber, G. (1971). *Inner-city children can be taught to read: Four successful schools.* Washington, D. C.: Council for Basic Education.

Weinart, R. A. (1987). Construction management: A sensible alternative when building new schools. *School Business Affairs, 53*(1), 16-21.

Williams, C. E. and Earthman, G. I. (1983). *The impact of selected variables upon school construction costs.* Paper presented at the Annual Meeting of the American Educational Research Association, Montreal, Quebec, Canada.

Williams, D. S. (1983). *Staff policy regarding migration of school enrollment impacts.* Sacramento, Calif.: Environmental Office, Siting and Environmental Division, California Energy Commission.

Wood, R. C. (1986). *Capital outlay and bonding.* Reston, Va.: Association of School Business Officials, International.

―――. (1988). Public policy in class action suits against school construction projects: Harber v. Franklin County School Board of Trustees. *West's Educational Law Reporter, 44*(1), 19-25.

Wright, D. L. (1983). Here's how one system built six new schools for the cost of five. *American School Board Journal, 170*(7), 32-33.

Yearwood, R. (1985). On-site design bridges the architectural gap. *American School and University, 58*(1), 66, 68, 73.

Zakariya, S. B. (1988). Construction is a hot, new board game with complex rules and gigantic stakes. *American School Board Journal, 175*(4), 27-30.

Appendix A: Additional References for Further Reading

Alcott, W. A. (1832). *Essay on the construction of schoolhouses.* Boston.

Baldwin, G. (1988). Fixed assets: Disposing of property and resulting funds. *Journal of Education Finance, 13*(3), 274-89.

Barnard, H. (1842). *Schoolhouse architecture.* Hartford.

———. (1850). *Practical illustrations of the principles of school architecture.* Washington, D.C.: G.P.O.

Boles, H. (1965). *Step by step to a better school facilities.* New York: Holt, Rinehart, and Winston.

Boyer, E. (1989). Buildings reflect our priorities, *Educational Record, 70*(1), 24-27.

Brooks, K., Conrad, M., and Griffith, W. (1980). *From program to educational facilities.* Lexington, Ky.: Center for Professional Development, College of Education, University of Kentucky.

Brubaker, C. (1988). These 21 trends will shape the future of school design. *The American School Board Journal, 175*(4), 31-33, 66.

Burrowes, T. H. (Ed.) (1855). *Pennsylvania school architecture.* Harrisburg.

Chase, C. T. (1868). *A manual on schoolhouses and cottages for people of the south.* Washington, D.C.: G.P.O.

Collins, G. (1987). Facilities outlook: School design, then, now, and soon to be. *American School and University, 59*(4), 12-13, 17-18.

Dwyer, C. P. (1856). *The economy of church, parsonage, and schoolhouse architecture adapted to small societies and rural districts.* Buffalo, N.Y.

Eveleth, S. F. (1870). *School-house architecture.* New York.

Garrett, D. (1981). *The impact of school building age on the academic achievement of high school pupils in the state of Georgia.* Unpublished doctoral dissertation, University of Georgia.

Glass, T. (1984). Planned maintenance program: A memorandum to facility officers. *Council of Educational Facility Planners Journal, 22*(3), 13.

─────. (1987). Demographic sources and data available for school district planners and architects. *Council of Educational Facility Planners Journal, 25*(2), 7-13.

Goldblatt, S. and Wood, R. (1985). Construction management for educational facilities: Professional services procurement and competitive bid statutes. ERIC Document, ED 268 670, 18 pp.

Graves, B. (1986). Facility planning: What do teachers want? *American School and University, 58*(8), 8.

Guthrie, J., Garms, W., and Pierce, L. (1988). *School Finance and Education Policy*, 2nd ed. Englewood Cliffs, N.J.: Prentice-Hall.

Harris, D., Burage, P., and Smith, W. (1986). Local insights to keep enrollment projections on the money. *The Executive Educator, 8*(11), 20-21.

Johonnot, J. (1859). *Country school-houses.* New York.

Klunker, C. (1987). Construction management and local contractors: A good team for the owners. *School Business Affairs, 53*(1), 22-23.

Klunker, C. and Haltenhoff, C. (1986). How to hire a construction management company. *School Business Affairs, 53*(5), 58-62.

Kowalski, T. (1983). *Solving educational facility problems.* Muncie, Ind.: Accelerated Development.

Lane, K. and Betz, L. (1987). The principal new to a school—What questions to ask about the facility. *National Association of Secondary School Principals Bulletin, 71*(502), 125-27.

Lewis, A. (1989). *Wolves at the schoolhouse door: An investigation of the condition of public school buildings.* Washington, D.C.: Education Writers Association.

Lows, R. (1987a). Enrollment Projection: A methodology for eras of growth and decline. *Council of Educational Facility Planners Journal,* 25(2), 4-7.

───. (1987b). School tax referenda: A case study of the relationship between referenda outcomes and demographic variables. *Journal of Education Finance,* 13(1), 30-44.

Piccigallo, P. (1989). Renovating urban schools is fundamental to improving them. *Phi Delta Kappan,* 70, 402-6.

Potter, A. and Emerson, G. B. (1842). *The school and the schoolmaster.* New York.

Pullum, T., Graham, S., and Herting, J. (1986). How to forecast public school enrollments. *American Demographics,* 8(10), 52, 54.

Quindry, K. (1979). The state-local tax picture. *Journal of Education Finance,* 5(1), 19-35.

Randall, G. P. (1866). *Descriptive and ilustrated catalogue containing plans in perspective of cottages, schoolhouses.* Chicago.

Roneau, E. (1989). The future of facility management. *Council of Educational Facility Planners Journal,* 27(1), 9-14.

Skypeck, W. (1988). Why ask for CADD? *Council of Educational Facility Planners Journal,* 26(6), 6-8.

Smith, E., Stevenson, K., Pellicer, L. (1984). Follow these nine steps to select the architectural firm that can design a new school to your exact specification. *The American School Board Journal,* 171(5), 36-37.

Smith, M. and Zirkel, P. (1988). Pauley vs. Kelley: School finances and facilities in West Virginia. *Journal of Education Finance,* 13(3), 264-73.

Spencer, D. (1988). Implications for facility planners at the elementary and secondary level. *Council of Educational Facility Planners Journal,* 26(2), 16-17.

Stewart, G. (1987). Confirming enrollment projections in rural districts. *Council of Educational Facility Planners Journal,* 25(2), 16-17.

Stollar, D. (1967). *Managing school indebtedness*. Danville, Ill.: The Interstate Printers and Publishers.

Sylvester, T. (1988). Relocatable and modular classrooms: Booming Business. *School Business Affairs, 54*(1), 22-27.

Uhler, S. (1988). Scrutinizing architectural contracts. *School Business Affairs, 55*(12), 57-58.

Winert, R. (1987). Construction management: A sensible alternative when building new schools. *School Business Affairs, 53*(1), 16-21.

Author Index

Abramson, P., 33, 52
Akers, S.B., 55
Albiani, G., 41
Alexander, L., 15, 38
Ambrosie, F., 39
American Association of School Administrators (AASA), 3, 25, 28, 29, 34
Anderson, C. S., 32
Augenblick, J., 39
Ayres, G., 56

Barnard, H., 26
Bell, C.S., 40
Birch, J.W., 28, 29, 33
Blair, B., 37
Boice, J. R., 14
Boles, H.W., 35
Bowers, J.H., 32
Boyer, E.L., 15
Brokaw, J.C., 51
Brubaker, C.W., 28, 49, 51
Burke, A.J., 33, 63
Burkett, C.W., 32
Burlingame, M., 29

California Coalition for Fair School Finance, 40, 41

California State Department of Education, 34, 37, 49
Cambron-McCabe, N.H., 40
Carter, M., 33
Castaldi, B., 25, 33, 37, 41
Chan, T.C., 51
Chang, V., 41
Chick, C.E., 40
Cold, B., 51
Coombs, F.S., 40
Council of Educational Facility Planners, 15, 27, 28, 35, 37, 49, 53, 57

Davis, J., 33
Day, C.W., 35, 37, 45, 46, 51, 52
Dressler, F.B., 27
Drexel, Burnham & Lambert, 42
Duke, D.L., 32
Dunham, A.G., 22

Earthman, G.I., 33, 35, 37, 51, 53, 54
Educational Facilities Laboratories, 14, 26
Education Writers Association, 40, 41
Eismann, D., 37
Elhanini, A., 51
Engelhardt, N.L., 20, 27, 37, 49, 55

Epperson, D.R., 53
Ernst, C.P., 123, 128
Evan, W.M., 16, 23, 148
Eveleth, S.J., 26
Everett, R.E., 46

Flagg, J.T., 32
Frederick, G.W., 48

Gipson, J., 40
Goldberg, W.H., 16, 23, 24
Goodlad, J.I., 15
Goodman, P.S., 23
Graves, B.E., 37, 39
Gump, P.V., 48

Hansen, S.J., 40
Haun, G., 51
Hawkins, H.L., 31, 55
Hedley, R.L., 51
Herron, P.L., 51
Hertz, K.V., 35
Hesse-Wallace, R., 41
Heydt, H.J., 5, 10
Hill, F., 35, 37, 56
Hill, J.C., 49
Holt, S.L., 47
Hudson, C., 40

Jenkins, J., 34, 37
Jilk, B.A., 53
Johnstone, B.K., 28, 29, 33
Jordan, K., 40

Karst, R.R., 31
Kaufman, H., 15-18, 34
Keck, D.B., 55
Keen, L.H., 15
Keith, P.M., 30
Keough, K.E., 37
Kimbrough, T., 39

King, D., 39
Kirschenstein, J., 41
Knirk, F.G., 47, 50, 53
Kowalski, T.J., 33, 57, 64
Kutkat, J.H., 50, 51, 53

Landes, J.L., 52, 55,
Leu, D.J., 15, 26, 30, 37
Lewis, M., 5
Lezotte, L.W., 32
Lilley, H.E., 55
Lindley, C., 48
Loveless, E.E., 33
Lowi, T.J., 16, 20, 22, 137
Lows, R.L., 37
Lutz, F.W., 56

MacConnell, J.D., 28, 34, 49, 53, 59, 95
MacKenzie, D.G., 34, 35
Mandel, D., 15
Manning, P., 46
Marmar, T.R., 22
Mayfield, J., 45
McClintock, J., 27
McClintock, R., 27
McGuffey, C.W., 31, 55
McQuaid, W., 46
Mills, E.D., 29
Minzey, J.D., 56
Miskel, C., 30, 32
Morocco, J.C., 32

New York State Department of Education, 32
Nisbet, J., 56

Ogawa, R., 30, 32
Organization for Economic Cooperation and Development, 25, 56, 57
Overbaugh, B.L., 31

Author Index

Palmer, A.M., 14
Passalcqua, J., 32
Pennings, J., 23
Perkins, D., 26
Perry, C., 32
Pierce, R.A., 43
Phi Delta Kappa, 30, 31
Plumley, J.P., 31
Price-Waterhouse, 12, 13, 14, 20

Reida, G.W., 55
Rosenbloom, C., 33
Roth, A., 25, 26
Rutter, M., 31

Samption, M.R., 52, 55
Seaborne, M.V.J., 46
Sinclair, R.L., 32
Sizer, T.R., 15
Smit, D., 41

Smith, L.M., 30
Speicher, A.D., 37, 45
Stewart, G.K., 56
Stone, A., 16, 20, 22
Strayer, G.D., 27, 55
Strevell, W.H., 33, 63
Swenson, E.S., 56

Taguiri, R., 31
Tanner, C.K., 49
Thompson, D., 39
Townsend, A.C., 56
Truby, R., 32
Tucker, M., 15

Walton, R.E., 16, 148
Weber, G., 31
Williams, D.S., 37
Wood, R.C., 38
Wright, D.L., 50

Subject Index

American Schoolhouse, 27; Dwight Perkins Carl Schurz High School, 26; Hillsdale Home School, 26
asset management, 38, 44
architect, 51, 89-94, 96, 99, 100, 103-107, 115, 137-139, 147-150, 154-156, 160. selection, 88
architectural form, 26, 28; Henry Barnard, 26; British infant schools, 48; campus, 28; cluster, 28; finger, 28; egg-crate, 31; Eveleth, 26; Greek revival, 26; Horace Mann, 26; Pestalozzi, 26; Quincy Grammar School, 28, 31; school designs, 33; Victorian, 26

bidding, 51, 52, 103-109, 159; architect, 103; bidding meeting, 105; construction management, 106; construction managers, 104, 159; contractors, 103; pre-bid conference, 104, 105, 159; subcontractors, 106
board member, 154, 155 (see school board)
building design, 46, 50, 88-90, 94-96, 99, 100, 103, 104, 107, 115, 116, 118, 131-133, 135; budget limitations, 110; floor plans, 48; relocatables, 95; 110; time limitations, 110;
building occupancy, 53; building dedication, 53, 54
building school facilities, 3; (see educational facilities, school facilities, schoolhousing)
building use, 56, 57; core, 56; educational facility planning in, 56, 57; escalating taxes, 57; plan and build, 56, 57

California Basic Educational Data System (CBEDS), 67, 70, 71, 76
California Educational Research Cooperative, 6, 79, 94
California facilities needs, 76; enrollment increases, 76; new development, 76; population displacement, 76; funding needs; general obligation bonds (GOBs), 76, 78-80, 83, 84, 86, 87; Mello-Roos, 76, 78, 85-87; funding plans, 76; developer fees, 76; 77; Proposition 13, 77, 79; developer fees, 82, 84, 86, 87; developers, 84, 86; independent district funding, 85, 86; LeRoy Greene Lease-Purchase

189

California facilities needs *(continued)*
Program, 86; redevelopment fees, 86; school sites, 86; special combination plans, 86; state funding match, 82, 84 (see matching funds); school construction, 12; California Legislature, 12; Price-Waterhouse, 12
California School Finance Authority, 38, 39
California State Department of Education/School Facility Planning Division (CSDE/SFPD), 11, 64, 74, 80, 81, 98, 143, 145, 147, 149, 150, 155, 161
certificates of participation, 44
Challman, Samuel A., 27
changes, 110-114, 117, 132-134; budget limitations, 110; building design, 112; building specifications, 113; change orders, 53, 114; contractor, 113; repairing, 132, 133; replacement, 132, 133; school construction, 110; state approval, 113, 114; subcontractor, 113; time limitations, 110
Charles McDermott (see McDermott)
Churchill, 30
Coalition for Adequate School Housing (CASH), 7
community growth, 71; community involvement, 34, 74, 83, 84, 135, 136, 160, 161; groundbreaking ceremony, 109; support, 123
construction of new schools, 52, 57, 58, 63, 66, 67, 74, 135, 136, 150
construction, 52; change orders, 53; construction management, 106, 107, 116; construction manager, 104, 117, 159; school facility, 4; plans, 138; process, 10, 19, 24, 25, 35, 66, 67, 74, 100, 101, 104, 105, 110-112, 115-117, 123, 157, 161; architectural services, 24; bidding and contracting, 24; budget limitations, 117; changes, 117; charette, 34; citizen involvement, 34; community involvement, 74; constructing the building, 24; contractor/architect relationship, 112; costs, 107 educational specifications, 24, 46, 47; executive planning team in, 33; fiscal planning, 24, 75; groundbreaking ceremony, 118; institutional planning team in, 33; interim housing, 119; long-range planning, 24; needs assessment, 24; occupying the building, 24; postoccupancy evaluation, 24; school building planning, 24; school costs, 47; school site planning and selection, 24; time limitations, 117; contracting, 51, 52, 103-109; architect, 103; bidding meeting, 105; construction manager, 104, 159; contract, 104; contractors, 103, 115-117, 156; general contractor, 51; multiple contracts, 52; pre-bid conference, 104, 105; subcontractor, 106; subletting, 104, 105
Council of Educational Facility Planners International, 27
county office, 69, 73

dedication of new school, 125, 127-129
Department of the Treasury, 78
design, 52, 56, 57, 94; architectural plans, 52; core, 56; mechanical features, 55 modification possibilities, 52, 53; specifications, 52; structural features, 55;
developer, 71, 84-86, 97, 98
developer fees, 41, 68, 69, 76, 77, 82, 84-86, 161; 201 developer fees, 41; Classroom Structure Authority (CSA), 85
development, 75, 86, 156
distributive, 20, 24, 59, 140; state

agencies, 16; technical assistance, 22; technical service, 140; policies, 16, 21, 22; relationship, 137, 140

educational facilities, 3 (see school facility, schoolhouse)
educational facilities laboratory, 14
educational facility planning, 56 (see CSDE/SFPD)
educational performance, 29 (see effective schools)
educational specifications, 45, 46, 50, 51, 54, 55, 88-90, 93-96, 99, 100, 143, 154, 155, 159; fire marshall, 81; fiscal conditions, 95; principal, 92, 94; regulatory conditions, 95; state regulations, 95; state standards, 90
effective schools, 29-32; egg-crate, 31; organizational ecology, 30, 31; physical plant characteristics, 30; school climate research, 32; smaller schools, 32
establishment of need, 73, 74 (see need for school facilities, facility need, need recognition)
evaluation instruments, 54, 55 (see postoccupancy evaluation)
executive function, 19, (see executive leadership)
executive leadership, 15-17, 24, 35-37, 45, 49, 51-55, 57, 58, 66, 73, 75, 79, 84, 87, 89, 94, 96, 99-101, 106-109, 113, 117, 118, 120, 124, 125, 128, 129, 134, 135, 153-158, 160; educational planner, 35; expanding building use, 56, 57
expressive meanings, 16, 24, 25; interpersonal, 23; relationship, 147, 148, 150, 155

facilities planners, 7, 33, 35, 63-70, 73-75, 79, 81, 82, 86, 87, 91, 96, 99, 106-108, 124, 129, 134, 135, 147-150, 154, 156, 160

facility construction, 9, 63, 64, 109, 110; construction process, 10; groundbreaking ceremony, 109; symbolic role, 9
facility need, 10, 67, 76, 87, 88, 158, 159
financial advisors, 39
fire marshall, 148
fiscal, 20, 22, 59, 141; allocation, 24; planning, 38, 75, 76, 80, 81, 87, 97, 136, 161; costs for school construction, 107; developer fees, 76, 77, 82, 84, 86, 87; developers, 84, 86; federal government, 76; general obligation bonds (GOBs), 76, 79, 80, 81, 83, 84, 86, 87; independent district funding, 85, 86; LeRoy Greene Lease-Purchase Program, 76, 77, 78, 86; Mello-Roos, 76-78, 85-87; Proposition 13, 77; redevelopment fees, 86; school sites, 86; special combination plans, 86; state funding match, 82, 84; relationship, 137, 142, 143, 145, 150, 155, 161, 162
floor plans, 48; campus, 48; circular, 48; cluster, 48; corridor, 48; courtyard, 48; finger, 48; loft, 48; open design, 48; funding, 57, 59
funding authority, 10; anticipation notes, 42; asset management, 38, 44; authorities, 40; bonds, 41; certificates, 44; community support, 41; construction, 5, 57; cost, 5; developer, 79; developer fees, 41, 161; escalating taxes, 57; finance formulas, 40; flat grants, 40; funding, 57; Government Obligation Bonds (GOBs), 86, 161; independent district, 85, 86; joint venturing, 44, 45; lease rental financing, 40; leasing, 42, 43; leasing programs, 39; LeRoy Greene Lease-Purchase Agreement, 43, 44; loans, 39; local taxation options,

funding authority *(continued)* 39; Mello-Roos, 42, 85, 86, 161; municipal leasing, 43; redevelopment fees, 161; sale of property, 44; sources, 39, 69, 75, 76, 158, 159, 161; special taxes, 41, 42; state grants, 39; tax increment, 44

gender, 156
general obligation bonds (GOBs), 40, 41, 76, 78, 80, 81-84, 87, 161; Proposition 13, 77
groundbreaking, 109, 110, 118

Horace Mann (see Mann)
horizontal interdependence, 145
housing of students, 110, 111

independent district funding, 85, 86
instrumental meanings, 16, 25; interpersonal, 23; relationship, 147, 148, 150, 155
interim housing, 119, 121, 122, 129; interim site, 123
interorganizational relationships, 16, 23, 24, 59, 145, 161; school district/state agency relationship, 24, 25
interpersonal interaction, 145, 147, 148, 149, 150, 155, 162; relationship, 59

joint venturing, 44, 45

Kalamazoo Court Decision of 1874, 26

landscaping, 48, 55, 94
lease-purchase agreements, 42, 43; certificates of participation, 44; leasing, 42, 43; municipal leasing, 43; leasing programs, 39; LeRoy Greene Lease-Purchase Agreement, 39, 43, 44, 77, 78, 86
local taxation options, 40; developer fees, 41; GOBs, 40
long-range planning, 37, 74, 75, 136, 143, 145, 153, 154, 159; enrollment projection, 37; shifting population, 75

manager of a project, 63, 64; (see project manager, management) facilities planner, 63-66
Mann, Horace, 26
matching funds, 82, 84, 87
McDermott, Charles, 27
Mello-Roos, 42, 76, 78, 85-87, 161 (See California funding)
movement of children, 119, 122-124, 129
move to new school, 121, 122, 123, 124; assignment of teachers, 121; children, 122, 123; purchase of equipment, 122

National Council on Schoolhouse Construction, 27
need for school facilities, 4, 10, 15, 67, 75, 76, 84, 87, 88, 158, 159; developers, 69; enrollment increases, 76; new development, 67, 76; new schools, 66, 67, 76; population displacement, 72, 76; relocatables, 72, 110; site acquisition, 97; recognition, 72 (see establishment of need), validation, 68, 69
needs assessment, 35, 67, 69, 70, 153, 154; classroom space requirement, 69; community involvement, 74; county office, 69, 70; developers, 69; displacement, 72; new schoolhousing, 71; relocatables, 95; site acquisition, 97

need sources, 67
new development, 67, 68-71, 74, 87, 88, 107, 158, 159; community growth, 71; county office, 69; county, 70; demographic data, 71; developer fees, 71; developers, 69, 71; long- range plan, 74, 75;
new school facilities, 28, 29; building, 9; construction, 135, 136; new facilities planning program, 85; schoolhousing, 71; long-range planning, 74, 75; architectural objects, 29; cultural statements, 29; educational performance, 30; physical plant characteristics, 30; learning conditions, 51; school designs, 33

occupancy, 53, 54; occupying the new building, 119; building dedication, 53, 54; new school, 124, 126-129
Office of Local Assistance (OLA), 74, 77, 81, 85, 140-143, 155, 161
Office of the State Architect (OSA), 77, 78, 80, 81, 85, 137-139, 140, 147-149, 155, 159, 161
opening new schools, 119, 120, 122, 123, 125-129; movement of children, 122, 123; purchase of equipment, 122
organizational processes, 155

parental support, 123
Pauley v. Bailey Court Case, 32
Pestalozzi, J. H., 26
political representatives, 16, 17; political legitimacy, 35
population displacement, 88, 158, 159; shifts, 74, 158, 159
postoccupancy evaluation, 54, 129, 132, 133, 134, 135; data-gathering instruments, 54; mechanical features, 55; structural features, 55
principal, 92, 93, 94, 121, 122, 123, 128, 130, 132, 133, 134, 135, 154, 155, 160; appointment, 120, 121, 124, 125, 129
professional agencies, 7; school legal defense, 7; professional function (see professional expertise), 19
professional expertise, 15-17, 24, 34-37, 45, 51-58, 73, 75, 79, 82-84, 87, 89, 90, 92-94, 96, 98, 100, 101, 104-109, 113, 115, 117, 118, 125, 128, 129, 132, 134, 135, 145, 147, 153-155, 157, 158, 160; architect, 97; construction management, 107; fiscal experts, 87; legal experts, 87; principal, 92, 94; relationship, 156
project management, 3, 63, 66, 100, 101, 153, 154, 156, 160; project manager, 63, 64; requirements, 4; school construction, 4; school projects, 64; special projects, 5
public administration, 18
public school construction, 5
purchase of equipment, 122, 124, 129

redevelopment, 80, 159; redevelopment fees, 161
redistribution, 24; redistributive, 20, 141; state agencies, 16; redistributive policies, 16; redistributive relationship, 137, 140
regulation, 24; regulatory, 20, 22, 24, 59, 141; state agencies, 10, 16; regulatory policies, 16; relationship, 137, 138, 139, 140, 142, 143, 145, 150, 155, 161, 162
relocatables, 72, 95
replacement; school facilities, 5
representative function (see representative legitimacy), 19, 56, 84, 96; representative leadership, 57, 58; representative legitimacy, 16, 17, 24, 35, 37, 38, 45, 51-54, 57, 73-

representative function *(continued)*
    75, 79, 81-84, 87, 89, 92-94, 96, 100, 101, 108, 109, 117, 118, 124, 125, 128, 129, 134, 135, 153-155, 157, 158, 160, 161; community involvement, 74; interagency planning process, 56, 57; school board, 19, 73, 74
research methodology, 6-8

sale of property, 44
school board, 73, 154, 155, 160
school building construction, 15 (see construction)
school building use, 24; educational facility planning, 56, 57
school construction, 16, 25, 47, 63, 66, 67, 74, 106, 107, 110, 111, 116, 117, 150, 153, 157, 160, 161; budget limitations, 110, 117; changes, 117; executive leadership, 15, 16; groundbreaking ceremony, 109, 118; historical development, 25; interim housing, 119; need for school facilities, 67; processes, 66, 155-158, 160, 161; professional expertise, 15, 16; project management, 4; representative legitimacy, 16; school projects, 64; state requirements, 109; time limitations, 117; long-range planning, 74
school district, 13; agenda, 12; interests, 12; interorganizational relationships, 16; interpersonal, 59; vertical interdependence, 16; staff, 10; state agency relationships, 59, 137-150, 155, 161, 162; interorganizational relationship, 23, 59; interpersonal, 23, 59; vertical interdependence, 23; facilities, 87, 88; learning, 31, 32; need for school facility, 5;
school facilities funding plans, 75, 76; school facility funding, 10, 95;

California Association of School Budget Officers (CASBO), 78, 79; Coalition for Adequate School Housing (CASH), 78, 79; costs for school construction, 107; developer, 76, 77, 84, 86; developer fees, 82, 84, 86, 87; GOBs, 76, 78, 79, 81, 83, 84, 87; LeRoy Greene Lease-Purchase Program, 76, 77, 78, 86; Local funding, 10, 11; Mello-Roos, 76-78, 86, 87; Proposition 13, 10, 11, 77, 79, 80; Schools Legal Defense Association (SLDA), 78, 79; Serrano v. Priest, 10; State School Building Lease-Purchase Act, 10, 11; (see funding) planning, 77; redevelopment fees, 86; school sites, 86; special combination plans, 86; state matching, 84
school facility need, 5; GOBs, 76; new development, 5; population shifts, 5; replacement, 5
school facility planning, 7, 16
school facility use, 16, 56, 135, 159; core, 56
School Finance Committee, 78
schoolhouse, 154, 155; egg-crate, 25, 26; first, 25; Quincy School, 25, 26, 28; planning, 27, 28; State Department of Education, 27; values, 6; schoolhousing, 25, 74, 156; construction, 6, 9, 10
School Legal Defense Association (SLDA), 78, 79
School Planning Laboratory, 14
school principals, (see principal)
school site, (see site); selection, 46, 49, 51, 70, 88, 89, 100; California State Department of Education/School Facility Planning Division (CSDE/SFPD), 98; site requirements and guidelines, 97; site acquisition, 97, 100, 143, 144
selecting the architect, 50, 51, 96; (see architect); cost-effective schools, 51

Subject Index

sharing school facilities, 135, 136
shifting population, 75
sources of funding, 87, 88 (see funding); need, 67, 158, 159, 161; new development, 67; replacement, 67 (see need)
special project, 5; school construction, 4, 5; school facility, 5; taxes, 41, 42
standards in American schoolhouses, 27
state agencies, 7, 10, 11, 22, 23, 64, 142, 155; agenda, 12; CSDE/SFPD, 12-14, 20, 24, 38, 49, 50, 80, 81, 98, 143, 147, 149, 150, 155, 161; California School Finance Authority, 87; Department of General Services, 11; 46, 47, 139; interorganizational relationships, 16, 59; regulations, 12; support services, 12; Department of the Treasury, 78; Director of Finance, 11; Office of Local Assistance (OLA), 6, 13, 14, 20, 23, 24, 28, 38, 43, 73, 74, 77, 81, 85, 140, 141-143, 145, 149, 150, 155, 161; Office of the State Architect (OSA), 11-14, 20, 24, 38, 77, 78, 80, 81, 85, 137, 138, 140, 145, 147, 150, 155, 159, 161; Price-Waterhouse, 13; school facility funding, 11; School Finance Committee, 78; State Allocation Board (SAB), 7, 11, 13, 14, 20, 23, 24, 28, 38, 43, 77, 78, 140-143, 145, 146, 150, 155, 161; vertical interdependence, 16, 59

state agency approach, 5
State Allocation Board (SAB), 11, 77, 78, 140, 141, 143, 145, 146, 150, 155, 161
State Department of Education, (see CSDE/SFPD)
state funding, 80 (see funding); grants, 39; state/local relationships, 20; regulations, 76, 77, 95, 113, 140, 141, 159; regulatory conditions, 95; site acquisition, 97; state inspector, 113; state requirements, 109; state standards, 90; support, 20, 137, 143, 149, 150
support relationship, 22, 150, 155, 161; symbolic, 24, 143, 145; technical, 24, 143, 145

tax increment, 44
teacher assignment, 121, 122, 124, 129
temporary buildings, 131; housing, 119, 122

use of school building, 56, 135, 136; core, 56; educational facility planning, 56, 57

vertical interdependence, 16, 23-25, 145-147, 150, 155, 161; identity conflict, 23

Woods, Frank H., 27
Wright, Frank Lloyd, 26, 50